DATE DUE

DELEGATION AND EMPOWERMENT: LEADING WITH AND THROUGH OTHERS

Michael E. Ward

with

Bettye MacPhail-Wilcox

EYE ON EDUCATION
6 DEPOT WAY WEST, SUITE 106
LARCHMONT, NY 10538
(914) 833–0551
(914) 833–0761 fax

Library of Congress Cataloging-in-Publication Data

```
Ward, Michael E., 1953-
   Delegation and empowerment : leading with and through others /
Michael E. Ward with Bettye MacPhail-Wilcox.
      p.    cm.
   Includes bibliographical references (p. ).
   ISBN 1-883001-76-5
   1. School principals--United States.   2. Delegation of authority.
I. MacPhail-Wilcox, Bettye.   II. Title.
LB2831.92.W37   1999
371.2'012'09730 01-19-99; sj05 01-21-99--dc21              99-17107
                                                              CIP
```

10 9 8 7 6 5 4 3 2 1

LB
2831.92
.W37
1999

Editorial and production services provided by Richard H. Adin Freelance Editorial Services, 9 Orchard Drive, Gardiner, NY 12525 (914-883-5884)

Also Available from EYE ON EDUCATION

Working in a Legal and Regulatory Environment:
A Handbook for School Leaders
by David Sperry

Human Resources Administration:
A School-based Perspective
by Richard E. Smith

Money and Schools:
A Handbook for Practitioners
by David C. Thompson and R. Craig Wood

The Principal as Steward
by Jack McCall

The Principal's Edge
by Jack McCall

The Reflective Supervisor:
A Practical Guide for Educators
by Ray Calabrese and Sally Zepeda

Thinking Through the Principalship
by Dianne Ashby and Sam Krug

Hands-on Leadership Tools for Principals
by Ray Calabrese, Gary Short, and Sally Zepeda

The Administrator's Guide to School–
Community Relations
by George E. Pawlas

Data Analysis for Comprehensive
Schoolwide Improvement
by Victoria L. Bernhardt

The School Portfolio:
A Comprehensive Framework for School
Improvement
by Victoria L. Bernhardt

Research on Educational Innovations (2d ed.)
by Arthur K. Ellis and Jeffrey T. Fouts

The School Leadership Library
David A. Erlandson and Alfred P. Wilson, General Editors

The School Leadership Library, a series of 21 books, shows you what successful principals and other school leaders must know and be able to do. Grounded in best knowledge and practice, these books demonstrate best practices of effective principals. They provide recommendations which can be applied to a school leader's daily work.

Each volume includes practical materials, such as:

- checklists
- sample letters and memos
- model forms
- action plans

What should an effective principal know and be able to do? Members of the National Policy Board for Educational Administration (sponsored by NAESP, NASSP, AASA, ASCD, NCPEA, UCEA, and other professional organizations) developed a set of 21 "domains," or building blocks, that represent the essential knowledge and skills of successful principals. Each volume in this series is dedicated to explaining and applying one of these building blocks.

Contact Eye On Education for more details.

The School Leadership Library

The Functional Domains

Leadership Gary M. Crow, L. Joseph Matthews, and Lloyd E. Mccleary

Information Collection Short, Short, and Brinson, Jnr.

Problem Analysis C.M. Achilles, John Reynolds, and Susan Hoover

Judgment James Sweeney and Diana Bourisaw

Organizational Oversight Erlandson, Stark, and Ward

Implementation Anita M. Pankake

Delegation Michael Ward and Bettye MacPhail

The Programmatic Domains

Instruction and the Learning Environment James Keefe and John Jenkins

Staff Development Sally J. Zepeda

Student Guidance and Development Ward and Worsham

Measurement and Evaluation James F. McNamara and David A. Erlandson

Resource Allocation M. Scott Norton and Larry Kelly

The Interpersonal Domains

Motivating Others David P. Thompson

Interpersonal Sensitivity John R. Hoyle and Harrison M. Crenshaw

Oral and Nonverbal Expression Ivan Muse

Written Expression India J. Podsen, Charles Allen, Glenn Pethel, and John Waide

The Contextual Domains

Working in a Legal and Regulatory Environment: A Handbook for School Leaders David Sperry

* Other titles to follow

ACKNOWLEDGMENTS

We wish to thank our families for their unwavering support. We are also grateful to our colleagues, friends, and students. They are our best collaborators, and their experiences brought life to the research and practice that undergird the propositions, illustrations, and application exercises in this book.

Special appreciation is extended to Wendy Combs for her assistance with background research and her design work on a number of the figures used in the book.

TABLE OF CONTENTS

ABOUT THE AUTHORS

Dr. Michael E. Ward is State Superintendent of Public Instruction in North Carolina. Prior to his election in 1996, he served as Executive Director of the North Carolina Standards Board for Public School Administration. Earlier posts include service as a teacher, high school principal, and local superintendent of schools. He was honored in 1994 as North Carolina's Superintendent of the Year.

A three-time graduate of North Carolina State University, Dr. Ward received the University's Distinguished Alumnus Award in 1997. He serves as an adjunct professor of educational leadership in NCSU's College of Education and Psychology.

Dr. Ward has been recognized for his leadership in school-based decision-making, empowering stakeholders, and setting high standards for students, teachers, and administrators. These topics, along with his research on teacher tenure and dismissal, are the source of a number of presentations and articles, both by and about Dr. Ward.

Dr. Bettye MacPhail-Wilcox is Professor Emeritus and former Head of the Department of Educational Leadership and Program Evaluation at North Carolina State University. She is past President of the American Education Finance Association from which she received the Outstanding Leadership and Service Award. At NCSU, she was awarded the Outstanding Service and Extension Award and founded the Hodnett Doctoral Fellowship in Educational Administration. She was named Outstanding Alumnus for Texas Tech University.

Prior to her service at NCSU, she was a manager in the industrial sector and served as a teacher and administrator in the public schools of Virginia. In Virginia, she also served as President of the Tidewater Administrators and Supervisors. She studied at James Madison, Old Dominion, and Texas Tech Universities.

PREFACE

The very existence of the 21 Performance Domains of the Principalship, the substance of the School Leadership Library, speaks to the complexity and comprehensiveness of the principal's job as we move into the twenty-first century. When the National Policy Board for Educational Administration first identified and described the 21 Domains, more than a few knowledgeable observers expressed their dismay at what, on the surface, seemed to be the operational definition of an impossible job. Many principals, who deal every day with the reality outlined by the performance domains, are inclined to agree. Most recognize, however, that although the job may seem to be an overwhelming challenge, it must be done. The principal's responsibility is to see that it is done well.

A theme running throughout the books in the School Leadership Library is that the job of the principal, while both comprehensive and complex, is not impossible. The principal cannot lead the school alone, nor should the principal try to lead it alone. Running the school is the responsibility of the school's leadership team, an organizational vehicle that should be accessible to each of the school's stakeholders. School leadership can be exercised in many different ways, in many different settings, and by many different people. There are four basic reasons for this position: (1) there is more that needs to be done in leading the school than can be done by a single leader or by a small group of people at the top of the school organization; (2) there is energy and knowledge distributed among the stakeholders that need to be harnessed for the good of the school (3) every school stakeholder has a vested interest in the leadership of the school and the right and obligation to contribute to it; and (4) significant involvement of school stakeholders in the leadership of the school empowers them and elicits their best contributions to the success of the school.

This volume by Michael E. Ward and Bettye MacPhail-Wilcox describes thoroughly and effectively how delegation and empowerment can be accomplished. They emphasize the need for shifting the focus from the task of the individual school professional to the task of the school. They examine the conditions for effective delegation and help the principal identify opportunities for delegation. They identify different levels of participant involvement in leading the school and assist the principal in matching individual competencies with task requirements.

The authors recognize the complexity of the delegation process. They describe how different contingencies impact the delegation process and how the principal can use these separate and combined contingencies to move the school toward fulfillment of its vision. Throughout the book the authors make use of real-life situations to illustrate the principles they propose. Relevant theory is integrated into practical direction for the principal.

Effective delegation and the resulting empowerment of school stakeholders underlie all 21 performance domains of the principalship. This volume is, therefore, fundamental to the principal's effective leadership of the school in every aspect of its operation. It shows, in a very practical way, how the principal can maximize the leadership resources of the school. Few of the principal's tasks are more basic.

David A. Erlandson
Alfred P. Wilson

INTRODUCTION

THE EMERGING EMPHASIS ON DELEGATION AND EMPOWERMENT

School leadership has become increasingly complex. This increasing complexity has been attended by a growing realization that it is neither possible nor desirable for school leaders to do it all when it comes to making and implementing decisions.

In spite of these emerging insights, some administrators prefer not to delegate tasks, or to delegate only a few or certain kinds of tasks. Effective delegation and empowerment takes considerable knowledge and expertise. For some school leaders, these challenges alone are sufficient to prevent engaging the talent and energy of people within the school. For others, particularly administrators who cling to control or who are minimally committed to the participation of others in decision-making, planning, and implementation, these challenges serve to affirm their reluctance—and provide cover for their resistance to the participation of others.

Quality delegation and empowerment are not easy. Thwarting participation and empowerment, on the other hand, is not so difficult. Examples of school leaders who are openly opposed to sharing power and leadership with others exist everywhere. There are other principals who maintain a facade of interest in empowerment, but who subtly undermine the efforts of participants, wear down the interest and efforts of others, and ultimately prevail on all, or nearly all, issues. The former are easy to identify and, in the current era of valuing participation by stakeholders, are seldom valued by local boards for very long.

The subtle saboteurs, however, are harder to identify, and are perhaps even more frustrating to people within the organization. Their efforts to undermine the participation of others are usually not overt; indeed, some may sincerely believe that they are genuine in their commitment to the empowerment of others.

However, their tendencies are made evident through their actions.

The following section explores some of the behaviors of school leaders who are insincere in their support of effective delegation, and who work to diminish the involvement and contributions of others. As the title implies, this is a "tongue in cheek" exploration of such behaviors but, hopefully, the message is instructive!

TEN TIME-TESTED WAYS TO DEFEAT DELEGATION AND ERADICATE EMPOWERMENT

1. Speak first, speak loud, speak long **No Way!**

When there are decisions to be made, tasks to be completed, and projects to be developed and implemented, communication is essential between school leaders and the individual or group involved. The communication skills of the administrator impact the quality of such work activities. Administrators who insist on being first to assert opinions, preferences, biases, and strategies risk stifling those of participants. Domination of the dialogue in decision-making, planning, and implementation by the leader not only frustrates participants, but can ultimately diminish the quality of the related decisions and work products.

None of this is to suggest that leaders should be passive, nor that they should abdicate the responsibility to clarify tasks, disclose parameters, or facilitate decision making, planning, and implementation processes. Chapters 4 and 7 review research and offer suggestions on leadership behaviors which undergird successful communication related to delegation and the empowerment of others.

2. Take for granted that everyone knows what they need to know.   **No Way!**

Effective decision-making and task completion often require special capabilities on the part of participants. Delegation is a poor leadership tool if leaders fail to consider the requisite knowledge and skills that participants need to accomplish that which is expected. Matching the right people to tasks and projects is a critical leadership function. Making investments in the capacity of organization participants is also essential to the processes of delegation and empowerment. Chapters 5 and 6 explore literature and offer ideas regarding the manner in which leaders assess the readiness, willingness, and ability of prospective participants.

3. Assume that capable individuals can auto-matically form capable groups.

The dynamics of work in groups pose additional challenges to the quality and timeliness with which decisions and tasks are managed. One should be able to assume that the manageability and the ultimate quality of a project will be enhanced by placing responsibility in the hands of a committee, team, department, task force, and so forth. However, even the most knowledgeable and competent individuals can become unproductive in a group whose members cannot get along, or that organizes its tasks poorly.

This is not to suggest that harmony and smooth sailing are always essential in group work. Indeed, there are circumstances in which conflict is not only unavoidable—it is, if well managed, entirely healthy. Capable and sincere school leaders recognize the delicate balance required for healthy group dynamics, and work to strengthen the group's capacity for productivity.

Chapter 7 examines selected literature on group dynamics in organizations, and offers suggestions on building the task-related proficiency of groups and the specific skills related to effective teaming.

4. Behave as though delegation is primarily about making your life easier.

The perspectives upon which administrators base decisions to share planning and tasks with others become fairly transparent over time. It is important for leaders to examine the motivations which underlie such determinations.

Administrators who consistently use delegation as a means of enhancing personal power, avoiding unpleasant tasks or dropping "hot potatoes" will not win the hearts of their colleagues in the building. Just as significantly, they may miss the point that delegation and empowerment are also opportunities for building the capacity of individuals, and the performance of the organization. Chapter 1 explores the "me" perspective, and the "we" perspective associated with delegation and empowerment.

5. Provide inadequate time and resources. **No Way!**

Even decisions and tasks that are delegated with the best of intentions and undertaken by the most able staff members will experience difficulty if adequate resources are denied for completion. The principal who consistently gives short notice of deadlines for projects to delegatees, or who fails to provide the needed materials, equipment, space, and information, while perhaps not actively sabotaging the project, is certainly not supporting quality in performance. Chapter 8 reviews research and offers suggestions on supporting the processes of delegation and empowerment through the provision of adequate time and resources.

6. Change the rules late in the game. **No Way!**

People who undertake a task or decision appreciate knowing in advance the parameters that may constrain their work. Administrators who fail to disclose such parameters will frustrate participants, and may make them wary of accepting future assignments. The failure may be the result of inadequate forethought on the part of the leader, or it may be a product of the leader's displeasure with the direction in which delegatees are taking a certain decision or task. Whatever the reason, the participants resent changes in parameters and the imposition of unexpected constraints.

Chapter 4 discusses the importance of clarifying tasks and disclosing parameters. Chapter 9 analyzes literature on jurisdictional issues related to delegation and empowerment and provides suggestions on the importance of disclosing parameters in advance.

7. Use policies, rules, and laws as camouflage **No Way!** for an autocratic disposition.

For the principal who is not inclined to share leadership, there are a variety of obstacles which can be cast in the way of persons who are otherwise willing and able to play a role in decision-making, planning, and task completion. A favorite ploy of such leaders is to raise authority constraints. Simply put, they use rules and regulations to frustrate the participation of others. For instance, it's easy to exclude teachers and parents from the process of selecting new staff members if the local personnel policy requires that the principal make the recommendation to the superintendent and the school board.

Examples of decisions and tasks around which constraints often exist include personnel issues, financial matters, and issues involving children with special needs. Principals are middle managers in most school organizations, and must deal with rules, regulations, and statutes. They are also frequently in the position of knowing whether such constraints are rigid or flexible. The degree to which a principal advocates for flexibility, and discloses flexibility opportunities to staff reveals a great deal about the principal's willingness to share decisions and engage others in meaningful tasks and projects. Chapter 9 examines the issue of authority constraints and offers suggestions on minimizing the negative impact of such constraints.

8. Keep it in "the club." **No Way!**

Some principals fall into the trap of always calling on the same staff members to help with important decisions, or to carry out important tasks and/or projects. The same tendencies may be evident in the choices such leaders make when asking parents to play a role in the decision-making and implementation processes of the school. It is natural to rely on people who consistently deliver, but playing favorites can breed resentment, harm a principal's effectiveness, and undermine the quality of delegation and participation.

The consequences of such leadership behavior can multiply. Those excluded from a role in planning and carrying out important tasks may develop a sense of alienation, and the broad support needed for critical decisions and projects may be withheld. There is also the risk of unfulfilled capacity; the leadership potential of other staff members and parents may go untapped. The opportunity to "share the load" may be missed, creating a sense of being unfairly burdened on the part of those who are so frequently selected.

Thoughtful administrators consider the interests and needs of stakeholders to be involved in meaningful ways. Chapters 3 and 5 examine research on the issue of task/decision relevance to stakeholders, and how it factors into decisions about delegation and empowerment of others.

9. Say "I told you so" when things go wrong.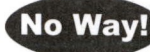

Contemporary discussions of the skills and knowledge needed for effective school leadership often highlight the importance of the participation of stakeholders. The unconverted leader may give lip service to valuing shared governance, but will often find ways to vindicate his or her belief that such a leadership philosophy is flawed. Thus, when problems arise in the quality of decisions and tasks that have been delegated, such a principal may engage in blaming the act of empowerment and/or berating the participants. While feedback and constructive criticism are important to improve communication and performance, they serve little purpose if they are merely a product of the principal's need to vindicate the assumption that the empowerment of others is risky.

Ultimately the propensities of leaders who are insincere in their support of delegation and empowerment become evident—and destructive. The leader who espouses a philosophy of empowerment should be genuinely committed because faculty members and parents will be eager to participate, and there will be no turning back. To paraphrase the old adage, such a leader must recognize that once the door to the participation of others is opened, he or she should be prepared to "dance with the bear until the bear gets tired." Chapter 10 explores the moral dimensions of school leadership behaviors associated with effective delegation of decisions and tasks.

10.Take credit for the hard work and successes of others.

This final strategy for undermining effective delegation and empowerment is a corollary of the ninth strategy—saying "I told you so" when things go wrong. Just as participants resent administrators who engage in blaming behaviors when delegated tasks encounter problems, they are also likely to resent principals who consistently fail to acknowledge participant contributions to the success of such tasks. School victories are often hard-won, and it is important to recognize and honor the contributions of staff and community members who have helped to generate successes. Failure to do so can generate frustration, diminish commitment, and harm the quality of the working relationship between the principal and the participants.

Some principals are prone to remind others that, although decisions and tasks can be shared, they are ultimately responsible for the outcomes. Aside from the basic unattractiveness of these reminders, such leaders fail to recognize that shared governance can actually serve to improve the prospects of success for the very decisions and tasks over which they have responsibility.

The leader who wants the school to succeed, and who wants to retain the commitment of staff and community to continued success, will place a premium on sharing the credit. Chapter 10 explores the moral dimensions of school leadership behaviors, including blame and credit, associated with effective delegation of decisions and tasks.

SUMMARY

Obviously, the preceding observations about leader behaviors paint a portrait that is almost entirely the *converse* of the principal who is needed for contemporary schools. The balance of this text explores the literature on delegation and empowerment. It delineates the significant variables that influence a leader's propensity to share the responsibility for decisions and tasks with others.

Perhaps most important are the practical suggestions on leadership behaviors that support effective delegation and empowerment. Wherever possible, anecdotes drawn from real-life school situations illustrate the practice of delegation, and offer you opportunities to expand your learning and to apply your knowledge. Sample questionnaires, strategies, and models are provided to lend some structure to the day-to-day practice of including others in the design and implementation of decisions and tasks.

It is our sincere hope that you will find this text to be a credible examination of the issues surrounding delegation and empowerment. More importantly, it is our wish that you find this material to be of real value as you work with others in our schools.

1

DELEGATION AND EMPOWERMENT ARE IMPORTANT AND TIMELY TOPICS

Finding ways to manage the demanding workload of school leaders is certainly not a new preoccupation among administrators. Assigning decisions and tasks to others has been practiced since hierarchical roles evolved in complex social organizations. However, in recent decades, school leadership has been characterized by a growing emphasis on the opportunities provided for those most affected by the decisions of administrators to play a significant role in shaping such actions.

Early management theorists largely discounted the notion of empowerment. Classical management theorists such as Frederick Taylor and Henri Fayol assumed that workers were motivated primarily by reward and needed close supervision if they were to be efficient in production (Hoy & Miskel, 1996). Human relations theorists such as Barnard (1938) and Simon (1947) introduced the zone of acceptance, a realm of decision making that workers are entirely comfortable leaving to management. These theorists also recognized another category of decisions that fall outside the zone of acceptance; these are decisions about which workers have considerable interest. They generally prefer to be included in making such decisions.

Recent years have witnessed a significant increase in the understanding and research of those issues upon which stakeholders wish to have some impact. Much of the theory and discussion about related practice is captured in the literature on school-based management—a management philosophy that is built around the concepts of delegation and empowerment.

Lewis (1990) identifies several contemporary trends that relate to the inclusion of stakeholders in the school community. Among the trends noted:

- More and more states are requiring some form of school-based leadership and stakeholder involvement in decision making and planning.
- School-based management is evolving from a program into a leadership philosophy.
- Broader participation among teachers and others is occurring on school management teams, or councils.
- School councils are taking on increasingly strategic roles in planning and implementation.

It is perhaps easier to determine that delegation and empowerment are important contemporary issues than to ascertain best practice in the area. Research affirms "that empowering others represents the biggest change and poses the most significant problems for principals" (Murphy, 1994a). Principals and other school leaders who want to involve others in decision making and implementation are frequently uncertain about how to proceed (Martin, 1990). Those willing to undertake the task may find that community and organizational attributes make it difficult for the principal to relinquish certain decisions and tasks (Murphy, 1994a).

It is for these reasons that this book was written. The text recognizes that skills in delegation and in the empowerment of others are essential from a practical perspective. We go further, however, for we also believe that there is an important ethical dimension to involving others in important decisions and in the completion of important tasks. There is a growing consensus that leaders are obliged to acknowledge the interest and potential contributions of stakeholders in the fulfillment of educational tasks, objectives, and missions.

WHAT ARE DELEGATION AND EMPOWERMENT? DELEGATED RESPONSIBILITIES VERSUS JOB DESCRIPTIONS

Delegation is the process of relinquishing decisions and tasks to others. Delegation can be a significant act of empowerment, for, in delegating, the school leader is relinquishing the responsibility to make a decision and/or complete a task personally. Delegation is one dimension of democratic leadership, which includes distributing responsibility among members of the school organization, empowering these members, and aiding their participation (Gastil, 1994).

For the purposes of this text, it is important to distinguish delegation from job designing or structuring. Decisions and tasks that are delegated are not ordinarily considered routine or ongoing in one's set of responsibilities. Decisions and tasks that *are* a regular part of one's job are usually considered elements of a job description. According to Thomas (1989), a job description is a form of delegation. The American Management Association contends, however, that once "ongoing responsibilities are delegated, it is no longer simple delegation; it is job designing or redesigning" (AMA, 1984).

This text describes how such distinctions are addressed when determining to whom and how decisions and tasks will be delegated.

WHAT IS THE RELATIONSHIP BETWEEN DELEGATION AND EFFECTIVE LEADERSHIP?

The school administrator's role has become increasingly complex and challenging. National and state studies of the roles and responsibilities associated with effective contemporary school leadership categorize administration in terms of domains, or dimensions, of effective practice. Virtually every such description of school administration identifies delegation and empowerment as important elements of effective leadership.

One of the most extensive descriptions of the contemporary school principalship was developed by the National Policy Board for Educational Administration. *Principals for Our Chang-*

ing Schools: Knowledge and Skill Base (Thomson, 1993), outlines 21 domains of the principalship. Delegation is cited as a key functional domain (Figure 1.1). The performance indicators acknowledge that effective leaders recognize their central role in organizations where "individuals and groups must work together to accept responsibility for performing tasks, solving problems, and achieving desired outcomes" (Thomson, 1993).

FIGURE 1.1. DELEGATION IS A FUNCTIONAL DOMAIN

The Principalship: Knowledge and Skill Domains
Source: *Principals for Our Changing Schools: Knowledge and Skill Base* (Thomson, 1993)

Functional Domains
1. Leadership
2. Information collection
3. Problem analysis
4. Judgment
5. Organizational oversight
6. Implementation
7. *Delegation*

Programmatic Domains
8. Instruction and the learning environment
9. Curriculum design
10. Student guidance and development
11. Staff development
12. Measurement and evaluation
13. Resource allocation

Interpersonal Domains
14. Motivating others
15. Interpersonal sensitivity
16. Oral and nonverbal expression
17. Written expression

Contextual Domains
18. Philosophical and cultural values
19. Legal and regulatory applications
20. Policy and political influences
21. Public relations

A second national study of the dimensions of school leadership was conducted by a multistate team known as the Interstate School Leaders Licensure Consortium (ISLLC). The third of six ISLLC standards is:

> A school administrator is an educational leader who promotes the success of all students by ensuring management of the organization, operations, and re-

sources for a safe, efficient, and effective learning environment (ISLLC, 1996).

The centrality of delegation and empowerment to effective leadership practice are evident in several of the performance indicators associated with this standard. Effective practice includes the administrator's capacity to facilitate processes and engage in activities which ensure that "stakeholders are involved in decisions affecting schools," and that "responsibility is shared to maximize ownership and accountability" (ISLLC, 1996).

Selected state studies of the dimensions of school leadership also point to the importance of delegation and empowerment. The North Carolina Standards Board for Public School Administration identifies as a key performance standard for principals and superintendents, the ability to "facilitate school improvement by engaging the school community's stakeholders in collaboration, team building, problem solving, and decision making" (Ward, 1996). Working "with stakeholders to set school improvement goals and plans for achieving them," and involving "stakeholders in school planning and decision making" are described as key indicators of proficiency related to this standard.

Other states have acknowledged the importance of delegation and empowerment in standards for the principalship. Colorado requires that a principal be able to demonstrate that the he or she "ensures that stakeholders are involved in decision making," and that he or she "empowers teachers, students, and parents to be leaders in the school community" (Principal and Administrator Professional Standards Board, 1994).

The state of California defines performance domains for educational administrators and articulates dimensions of leadership that support quality delegation and empowerment (California Commission on Teacher Credentialing, 1995), with statements such as:

- ♦ The [school leadership] candidate develops the ability to facilitate shared decision making among members of the school community.
- ♦ The [school leadership] candidate understands governance roles and has opportunities to practice

consensus building, develop collaborative relationships, and engage in team building activities.

♦ The [school leadership] candidate demonstrates the ability to make appropriate personnel assignments and recognizes the importance of each employee's skills, abilities, and training.

These are a sample of states that have developed standards for school leadership, which stress the importance of empowerment. It seems clear that a strong consensus exists supporting the notion that delegation and empowerment are critical dimensions of effective school leadership. We turn next to reasons that theorists and practitioners view the ability to give authority for decisions and tasks as being so important.

WHY DELEGATE?

THE "ME" PERSPECTIVE—"HOW *I* CAN GET *MY* WORK DONE"

According to Dyer (1983), the need for personal assistance is a consideration that typically underlies a school leader's decision to delegate to others. The lack of time, skills, and other resources often prompts the delegation of decisions and tasks. Speaking more specifically to school leadership, Hedges (1991) asserts that a lack of skill in delegation is one of the most significant time wasters for principals. Kergaard (1991) suggests that because principals often lack personnel support, delegation of responsibilities to others is essential to effective management of their time.

The motives underlying a decision to pass along a decision or task are sometimes a product of genuine reluctance on the part of the school leader to be associated with a sensitive matter. Delegation is sometimes undertaken to unload a difficult issue or a controversial project. And sometimes, although rarely, it is actually in the best interests of the organization for a controversial decision or task to be handled by someone other than the school leader.

Given the complex and dynamic nature of school administration, justifications for delegation such as those outlined in the previous two paragraphs are certainly reasonable. But these rationales are, at least in part, steeped in personal and professional self-interest. There are other important reasons to delegate which focus on the benefits to members of the organization, and to the organization itself.

THE "WE" PERSPECTIVE—"HOW *WE* CAN GET THE WORK OF THE ORGANIZATION DONE"

There are emerging perspectives on leadership that suggest that there are additional rationales for delegation which focus on empowering others within the organization. With the growing emphasis on empowerment of stakeholders and school-based decision-making, it is important to think beyond delegation as something a manager "does to others" (Scott & Jaffe, 1991). A prudent school leader will recognize that delegation has tremendous potential to build capacity in others, as well as to enhance the achievement of important organizational aims.

Teachers and others view an assignment more favorably when they believe that the aim of the task is to benefit others, and not just to benefit the principal, or simply to give the principal the opportunity to assert authority (Blase & Kirby, 1992). Dyer (1983) asserts that a strong rationale for delegation is often the school leader's desire to give members of the organization greater responsibility in order to provide them with an opportunity to learn and grow professionally. In addition, Thomas (1989) suggests that organizational effectiveness and productivity are enhanced by delegation. Thus, it seems evident that delegation must necessarily take on a rationale that goes beyond the immediate and personal stake that the school leader has in getting his or her work done.

WHAT'S AHEAD

The following chapters address the topics of delegation and empowerment from the practitioner's perspective. This approach renders the text as useful as possible to aspiring and practicing school leaders. Each chapter includes some combination of vignettes, guides, work-based documents, self-analysis instruments, and other assessments.

The practical orientation of the text does not ignore the critical nature of the theories that undergird effective practice in the areas of delegation and empowerment. An emphasis on practicality does not preclude an examination of theory; indeed, few things are more practical than well-founded, well-researched theories that help one to understand and even predict the consequences of certain behavior among individuals in organizations. With this in mind, we introduce pertinent theories in each chapter, along with research findings related to the chapter's topics.

Each chapter represents a synthesis of contemporary thinking on important dimensions of delegation and empowerment. Chapter 2 examines the nature of school administration, which is multidimensional and demanding. The chapter proposes a model that details the roles, functions, tasks, and responsibilities inherent in school leadership. Here, we make the case that, given the demanding nature of school administration, delegation and empowerment are not only essential to effective practice but such skills may well be *survival* skills for the practitioner!

Chapter 3 examines theories and models that propose strategies for effective delegation. From the models, factors impacting delegation and empowerment are synthesized, yielding six categories of delegation factors, or contingencies.

Chapters 4 through 9 examine each of these categories of delegation contingencies in detail, with practical guidance offered to steer the practitioner in factoring such contingencies into decisions regarding delegation.

Chapter 10 summarizes the previous chapters and proposes a synthesis model of delegation contingencies, with suggestions for pulling all of the variables together to systematically make quality determinations regarding when, how, and to whom decisions and tasks might be assigned.

APPLYING YOUR KNOWLEDGE

1. Review the school leadership perspectives discussed in the sections entitled "The 'Me' Perspective or 'How *I* Can Get *My* Work Done,'" and "The 'We'

Perspective or 'How *We* Can Get the Work of the Organization Done.'" Consider the vignettes below. Which delegation perspective appears to be evident in the behavior of the individual in each scenario? What reasons support your response?

- Vignette 1: James Averette is principal of West Berkeley Middle School. He has become concerned about the increasing noise level and rowdiness of students during lunch. He has decided to bring several members of the coaching staff in and have them perform monitoring and supervisory duties in the cafeteria.

- Vignette 2: Funding for materials, equipment, and supplies is assigned to each school in Prince Helen's County on the basis of student enrollment. Maria Delgado is Martin High School's principal, and has just received the projected allotment amounts for the coming school year. She has asked department chairs to meet with her to determine jointly the expenditure priorities and allocations across departments and program areas.

- Vignette 3: The principal and staff at Apple Gate Middle School are interested in getting parents involved with their children's teachers and with the total school program. Principal Evelyn Mason is aware of the typical decline in parent involvement as students get older, and is unsure of the best strategies to pursue. She invites a group of parents, who are representative of the school's diverse population, to work with staff members to develop and implement proposals to fulfill the goal of increased parental involvement.

- Vignette 4: James Barnhill is the principal of Madison Elementary School, a school to which an assistant principal is also assigned. James has worked with a number of assistant principals over the years. He routinely assigns the assistant principals with whom he has worked such duties as supervising transportation services, ordering supplies, managing textbooks, and dealing with students who are referred for discipline. None have been involved in strategic planning, scheduling, working with teachers on instructional issues, and dealing with parent and community involvement, which are responsibilities that James has consistently reserved for himself.

2. Review the leadership domains outlined in the various national and state models of effective school leadership practice. Discuss with your colleagues or classmates the relative impact you believe delegation has on overall administrative effectiveness as contrasted with other leadership dimensions.

EXTENDING YOUR KNOWLEDGE

Locate a copy of either of these texts:

Thomson, S. D. (1993). *Principals for our changing schools: Knowledge and skill base.* National Policy Board for Educational Administration. Lancaster, PA: Technomic Publishing Co.

Interstate School Leaders Licensure Consortium (1996). *Standards for school leaders.* Washington, DC: Council of Chief State School Officers.

and examine the sections that address issues related to delegation and empowerment. The review will enhance your understanding of the perspectives of the various authors on the importance of delegation and empowerment, and strengthen your insights into the skills, knowledge, and professional perspectives that undergird effective practice in these important leadership domains.

2

THE SIGNIFICANCE OF DELEGATION IN ADMINISTRATIVE PRACTICE

SETTING THE STAGE

THE SITUATION

When Ms. Brookneal arrived at the school on Monday morning, the school secretary presented her with a stack of mail 8 inches high, a list of 10 phone calls, and briefed her on the status of the 4 persons sitting in the waiting area of the main office. Mr. Jones, the janitor, hailed her as she turned to enter her office and informed her that the "flashings on the building were so deteriorated that the roof over the north side of the gymnasium had rotted." He reminded her hurricane season was approaching and that the bleachers, where students and community members sat, were directly under the rotting roof section.

Ms. Brookneal thanked Mr. Jones and asked him to estimate the materials, labor, and time needed for the repair, and to give her the estimates by the next day. As she neared her office, the Superintendent's secretary called, wanting to know, before the reporters called, the status of students involved in the bus incident this morning. Ms. Brookneal had not yet read the message from the driver of bus 101, which stated that two students had been involved in a fight with several other teenagers at their bus stop and that both were taken to the hospital.

As Ms. Brookneal was assuring the Superintendent's secretary that she would get the facts and report back as quickly as possible, Mr. Seratti appeared at her door and reminded her that today is the day she is to meet with teachers in the math department during the first period common planning time to decide which computerized remedial math program to purchase.

Just then, the secretary interrupted Mr. Seratti to remind Ms. Brookneal that four parents were waiting to see her about a suspension, a teacher complaint, a program placement issue, and her plan to limit the boosters' involvement in school sales.

Ms. Brookneal remembered that this week she had planned to conduct informal observations of at least 30 of the 72 staff members. She also thought about how she had hoped to use these early hours to prepare for her presentation to the Lion's Club today. At this meeting, she hoped to build support for the school's academic program and her mission to insure that "every child succeeds at Sweeney High School." She sighed briefly when she remembered that today is also the day that she is to inaugurate a series of "school-town council meetings," to learn what the community perceives Sweeney's needs, strengths, and opportunities for improvement are. Today is also the day that she is to meet with a teacher who is likely to be dismissed and the teacher's attorney.

YOUR THOUGHTS ARE?

How would you describe this administrator's work? What skills, knowledge, and attitudes does a person need to perform effectively in the above situation? How do you imagine that this situation affects Ms. Brookneal? How does the nature of the job impact the effectiveness and efficiency of the school? How would you advise Ms. Brookneal to manage this kind of work environment? What do you recommend as potential strategies for handling these job demands?

THE NATURE OF ADMINISTRATIVE WORK

It would hardly make sense to pursue a profession, career, or job without a strong sense of what the work is like and the degree of compatibility between one's own attributes and the work. If the introductory situation described here seems overwhelming to you, you are in good company. Scholars who study managers and school administrators (Currie & Rhodes, 1991; Gronn, 1982; Mintzberg, 1973; Pitner, 1988; Pitner & Ogawa, 1981; Wolcott, 1973) using "shadowing" or observer data collection procedures, report that administrative work:

- Is overwhelmingly constituted of communication, especially oral forms, that consumes 50 to 90% of the executive's time.

- Is high in volume, filled with active, discrete problems, such that each is assigned brief periods of time, executed at an unrelenting pace, and punctuated by frequent interruptions.

- Requires working relationships with three primary groups: superiors, subordinates, and outsiders.

- Is perceptually preoccupying, in that the manager is never free from the position, nor from the thoughtful analysis, planning, and information seeking activities of the mind.

- Occurs in very uncertain political and technical knowledge environments.

Clearly, time and energy are critical and severely constrained resources for school administrators. The time, energy, and expertise demands placed on a school administrator are readily apparent in other descriptive studies of educational administration, some of which are systematically summarized in the tridimensional model in Figure 2.1.

Descriptive literature on management and administration illustrates that administrators assume multiple roles ranging from leader and figurehead to negotiator (Getzels & Guba, 1957; Mintzberg, 1973; Pitner & Ogawa, 1981). Roles are personal, institutional, and group expectations for identifiable sets of social behaviors.

In addition to the wide array of roles administrators are expected to assume, they are assigned numerous responsibilities including management of fiscal, personnel, and programmatic areas (Kimbrough & Nunnery, 1988). Job responsibilities are

FIGURE 2.1. A TRI-DIMENSIONAL MODEL OF EDUCATIONAL ADMINISTRATION

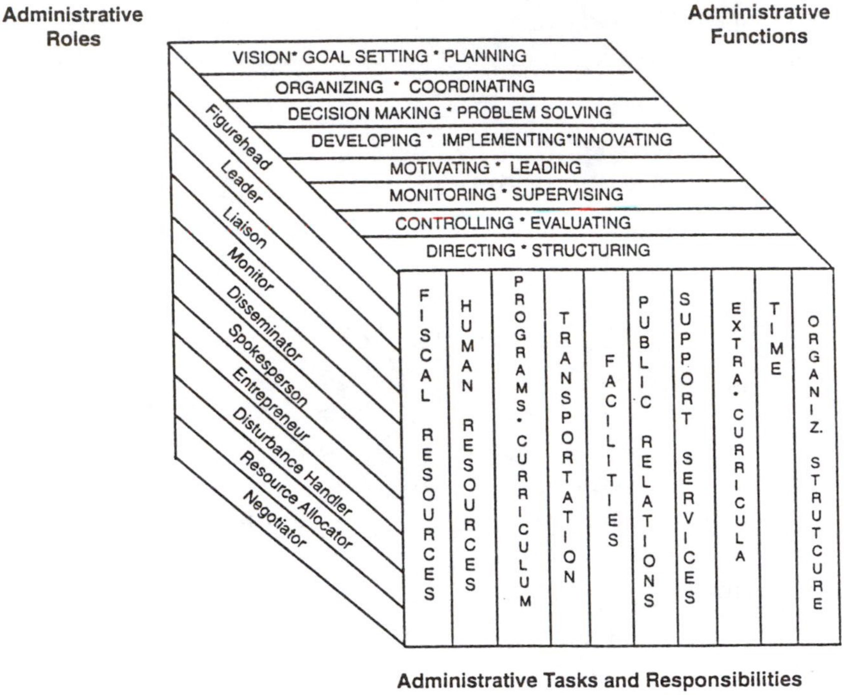

Administrative Tasks and Responsibilities

identifiable parts of a whole job for which one is held account-able. They are apparent in job descriptions, legislation, adminis-trative assessment tools, and research.

Within these multiple roles and responsibilities, administrators are expected to execute a broad array of administrative functions from planning to evaluating (Gulick, 1937). These functions may be thought of as clusters of related tasks pertinent to each area of assigned responsibility. In other words, administrators are required to execute each administrative function within each of the areas of assigned responsibility.

One means by which the workload, job demands, and complexity of a school administrator's job can be synthesized is by cross-classifying these three related dimensions of administrative jobs. We call the resulting cube the Tri-Dimensional Model of Educational Administration (see Figure 2.1). This model provides a comprehensive synthesis of administrative job demands which may be explicit in statute and policy, or implicit in hiring, longstanding practices, and expectations.

Without question, this model illustrates how difficult it is for a single actor, the school administrator, to accomplish all that needs to be done in the management of a school unit. One of the strategies by which some administrators optimize their time is through the use of delegation (Cooper, 1988).

An understanding and effective use of delegation are essential to the success of school leaders. Beginning principals report that delegation is a significant challenge for them (Lyons, 1993). The challenge is exacerbated by the fact that models of delegation as an administrative practice are largely limited to exhorting administrators to be mindful of the need for it and the potential pitfalls associated with it.

For example, one comparison study of principals and public sector supervisors ranked delegation thirteenth and sixteenth, respectively, of 19 key functions for administrators and managers (Fields, 1982). Yet, the tri-dimensional model plainly illustrates how essential delegation is to the efficient accomplishment of administrative work.

In addition, there are other important contemporary leadership issues that make delegation essential. Among these contemporary perspectives are the growing tendencies of administrators to promote the empowerment of staff and communities, and the devolution of decision authority via school-based management, self-governing teams, and broadened participation in school-community decisions (Lindquist & Mauriel, 1989).

RELATIONSHIP BETWEEN DELEGATION AND EMPOWERMENT AND CONTEMPORARY LEADERSHIP ISSUES

Schools have been widely criticized during the last two decades as ineffective in their academic mission and have been blamed for the trends of economic decline in this country (Finn, 1992). Communities contend that student performance is not adequate and that schools are unresponsive to community needs. Teachers retort that they are not empowered by administrators to improve student performance, and research supports the charge (Sousa, 1982). Administrators respond that they are not empowered by school statutes and school board policies with enough authority or flexibility to improve schools (MacPhail-Wilcox, Forbes, & Parramore, 1990).

Yet school reformers claim that teacher and community empowerment are critical pieces in the school improvement puzzle. This assertion rests on the belief that empowerment can unleash the most relevant and practical knowledge and bring it to bear on school process problems. It can thus lead to better ways to organize and operate schools so that the performance of all students will be improved (Hallinger, 1992; Herman, 1991; MacPhail-Wilcox & Alford, 1988; White, 1990). Empowerment through teams can increase the psychic, technical, and sociopolitical resources of the school significantly enough to focus attention on recalcitrant problems and to bring about significant adaptive action (Maeroff, 1993). But it does not always do so; empowerment requires the *real* delegation and redistribution of authority to be effective (Duttweiler & Mutchler, 1990; Lindquist & Mauriel, 1989; Wohlstetter & Odden, 1992). Yet principals acknowledge that in this period of transition they are finding it difficult to manage the balance between control and delegation (Corcoran & Wilson, 1985; Lindquist & Mauriel, 1989).

It is not surprising that the most commonly recommended systemic strategy for empowering school professionals and communities is a performance-team oriented strategy called school- or site-based management (SBM). SBM is viewed as a means to a set of ends, usually improved student performance and enhanced teacher morale (Seeley, 1991). It is a structure and a set of processes that enable school stakeholders to collaborate in school problem-solving and decision-making in order to improve performance. Hence, SBM schools are learning organizations (Dixon, 1995; Isaacson & Bamburg, 1992) in which persons closest to performance processes and problems (i.e., teachers and principals) analyze existing conditions as a basis for developing, implementing, and evaluating a shared future vision of schools (Leithwood, 1992; Tye, 1993). The school community becomes a dynamic learning unit, as teams collectively search for performance problems, then conceptualize and implement improvement solutions which can be evaluated for effect.

Delegation is an administrative process that can enhance teacher empowerment. When appropriately implemented, it can reduce the unproductive and enduring isolation of insight and knowledge that have characterized the internal and external relationships in schools (Cuban, 1988). The term "appropriately implemented" is intended to distinguish between thoughtfully planned delegation and the forms of delegation that coexist with administrative neglect.

Empowerment is experienced as the result of being invested with the power, authority, means, knowledge, and opportunity to be or do something perceived as important. Delegation has been defined as "assigning projects, tasks, and responsibilities with clear authority to accomplish them in a timely and acceptable manner; utilizing subordinates effectively; following up on delegated activities" (Muse, Hite, Smith, Matthews, & Britsch, 1993, p. 7-3). When a capable employee is delegated an operation with appropriate responsibility and resources with which to accomplish the operation, they are *empowered* to contribute or develop their skill and knowledge toward the accomplishment of something important to the welfare of students, fellow employees, and the school.

Job characteristics theory (Hackman & Oldham, 1976) reports that when employees are empowered they experience work as meaningful and feel responsible for the quality of work outcomes. These psychological states, assuming a capable employee, lead to higher levels of work motivation, growth, job satisfaction, and work effectiveness. Blase (1987) found that effective principals readily delegated authority to teachers.

Appropriate delegation has potential to empower teachers and communities to renew or revise school goals, to improve student performance, and to enhance teachers' psychosocial work benefits (Huddleston, Claspwell, & Killion 1991; Imber & Duke, 1984). The term "appropriate," in the context of job characteristics theory, urges administrators to be mindful of the unique knowledge, skills, and growth needs of the employee.

Similarly, expectancy theories of motivation alert administrators that effective delegation requires considerable prior analysis. Administrators using this theory must analyze the degree to which the work delegated is attractive in terms of the direct and indirect outcomes (Vroom, 1964), as well as the specific task demands and employee perceptions of their capability to execute the demands effectively. Lewis (1987, 1989) clarifies the kinds of resources that affect an employee's perception of capability. Information, funds, materials, space, time, and support are essential resources for effective empowerment.

Total Quality Management (TQM) is a system and philosophy of management that, like SBM, has penetrated education as a reform intended to improve school performance. The founder of TQM, W. E. Deming (Walton, 1986), contends that management should be analytic. That is, good managers engage themselves and others in a continuous process of describing and improving all organizational processes in order to improve results. Consistent with SBM, TQM empowers individuals and teams to work across staff areas as they actively accomplish the transformations indicated as needed by performance data. In other words, employees are empowered and dedicated to a constant purpose of improving products and services.

Administrators using TQM systems must lead, delegate, coordinate, and support the continuous use and evolution of quality processes by an empowered work force. This is no small challenge and numerous private sector TQM efforts have failed because of the absence of real commitment and dedication to the pursuit of quality (Schaaf, 1991). The commitment and dedication must traverse the depth and the breadth of the entire system as well as reach to and include external consumers and suppliers (Walton, 1986). Even as they acknowledge such requirements, many school administrators contend that legislation and policy obstruct their efforts to empower schools and communities to achieve significant school improvement (MacPhail-Wilcox et al., 1990). In other words, the rules, regulations, and policies that govern schools remain tethered to the bygone industrial era. Consequently, legislators, boards of education, and administrative superiors do not evidence real commitment and dedication to the pursuit of quality.

Despite these barriers to change, administrative mastery of delegation is essential to the effective and efficient operation of schools. It is equally critical in the successful implementation of empowerment reforms like SBM and TQM.

SUMMARY

The job demands in educational administration, public dissatisfaction with school responsiveness and performance, and increasing emphasis on empowerment and SBM constitute powerful driving forces for administrative delegation. Each of these forces is premised on the belief that creativity and knowledge must be unleashed if we are to foster a continuous cycle and systemic approach to school improvement.

In constantly adapting learning communities, administrators will find it essential to share leadership by delegating responsibilities, tasks, and decisions to persons with the insight and informational resources to accomplish the work effectively. Thus, it is not surprising that the National Policy Board for Educational Administration (Thomson, 1993) includes delegation among the functional domains of knowledge and skill required of all administrators.

Effective delegation requires much more than just assigning an individual or team a task. It requires action based on a thoughtful analysis of "delegation contingencies," which are addressed in the chapters that follow.

APPLYING YOUR KNOWLEDGE

1. Shadow one or more principals during the same part of the day and code their minute-to-minute activities using the Tri-Dimensional Model of Educational Administration.

or

Interview two or more principals using the Tri-Dimensional Model of Educational Administration. Identify and code the role-function-task blocks that reflect the level of activity the administrator reports for the previous week. Various shading codes can be used to reflect a high, moderate, or low level of activity.

2. Interview a principal, a business manager, and a public administrator to find out how they delegate, why they delegate, and any special considerations they make when they are deciding to delegate.

3. Apply the five selected findings from descriptive research about the nature of administrative work to an analysis of the Ms. Brookneal's situation.

4. Interview a principal working in a "traditional" school and one working in a TQM or SBM school and compare the types of activities they delegate, how they delegate, and why. Extend your insight by asking the principals for permission to meet with selected teachers and interview them briefly about their perceptions of the types of activities they are delegated at work and the kinds of tasks for which they wish to have decision input.

3

THEORETICAL MODELS THAT PROPOSE STRATEGIES FOR EFFECTIVE DELEGATION

SETTING THE STAGE

THE SITUATION

Jan Mills has just been named principal of Central Middle School, which is presently under construction and which will be opened in the fall. Jan will come to this new role from the principalship at Willow Springs Elementary School which had 20 teachers and 300 students. Jan has been Willow Springs' principal for 8 years and has a staff that places its trust in her for most of the major decisions affecting the school. She visits classrooms daily and remains in such close contact with staff members that she generally has the information needed to make reasonably good decisions.

At Central, Jan will need to hire 75 teachers and all of the support services staff for a student body of 1,350. Central will be the first real middle school in the county, and it will be organized in interdisciplinary pods. All of the staff members will be chosen 6 months before the school opens, although most will not report until early August.

A number of the staff members at Central will be hired and transferred from within the district's existing teaching and support staff forces. Some new teachers will be hired as well. The local school board historically supports hiring from within whenever possible.

Hiring new staff members is not the only challenge facing Jan. There is no integrated middle school curriculum in the district and much of the instructional program must be developed.

Jan has a keen professional interest in the concepts of site-based management and staff empowerment. She would like to operate Central Middle School using management practices consistent with these concepts, even during the planning and setup phases. The board of education is skeptical of these ideas, but is willing to give Jan some latitude, as long as the school is "fully prepared to serve its students effectively and efficiently on opening day."

YOUR THOUGHTS ARE?

Imagine yourself in Jan's position. What kinds of decisions and tasks should Jan consider delegating? Why? What kinds of decisions and tasks should not be delegated? Why? Examine your responses and identify the factors that you believe Jan is implicitly considering as she makes decisions about what to delegate, to whom to delegate, when to delegate, and how to delegate.

Keep your responses to this activity on hand for use with exercises under Applying Your Knowledge at the end of the chapter.

INTRODUCTION

For those who believe that literature for educational leaders should focus on the real world, a palpable shudder may be felt upon reading the title of this chapter. As the situation described in Setting the Stage illustrates, we seek to provide a practical, hands-on guide to delegation. Such practical knowledge is based on the theoretical underpinnings of successful delegation. We intend, however, to show the relationship of such theory to the world of practice. With this in mind, Chapter 3 explores selected literature on delegation, decision making, and decision implementation.

Selected models, which describe decision making and delegation, are summarized so that key variables associated with decision making and delegation are identified. These variables are summarized and placed in a classification scheme throughout the chapter. They are combined later with leadership variables to illustrate how an administrator might behave in various delegation situations. Other theories are presented and integrated in later chapters.

ADMINISTRATION: MAKING AND IMPLEMENTING DECISIONS

Chapter 2 concluded that effective school leadership is demanding and complex, and requires an enormous amount of talent, energy, time, and expertise. The ability to make good decisions is a particularly critical area of expertise. School administration is, at its core, a process of decision making. Whether one is selecting a new staff member, considering instructional software, determining the appropriate consequences for a student's misconduct, or deciding how to respond to a bomb threat, an administrator makes choices and sees to their implementation at a relentless pace. Thus, few administrator capabilities matter more than those associated with making and implementing effective decisions.

Decisions about delegation are those that focus on to whom and to what extent others will be given decision making and decision implementation authority. Leader behavior in decision making and decision implementation will affect the level of member participation. Four variations in the level of participation prompted by the leader are described in Figure 3.1.

The ability to determine the mode of leader behavior appropriate for a given decision or task is an essential leadership skill. In fact, decisions about delegation are among the most important decisions made by administrators. To make effective decisions in this area, school leaders must be well-grounded in strong theories about decision making and delegation.

A number of individuals have developed pertinent theoretical models, some of which analyze the variables associated with shared decision making and delegation, some of which offer prescriptions for effective inclusion and delegation, and some of which do both. The next section explores a number of these models.

FIGURE 3.1. A HIERARCHY OF PARTICIPANT INVOLVEMENT

Level 1: The leader makes a decision and performs tasks without input from others:

Level 2: The leader gathers advice and opinions from others before making a decision and/or performing tasks:

Level 3: The leader participates as a member of a group which generates a decision and performs tasks:

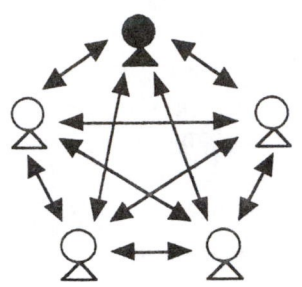

Level 4: The leader assigns the responsibility for making a decision and performing tasks to individuals or groups:

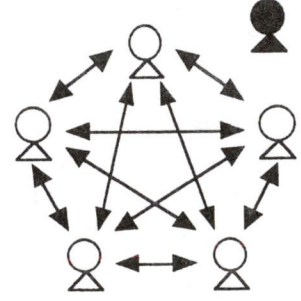

THEORIES OF
DECISION MAKING AND DELEGATION

HERBERT SIMON AND EDWIN BRIDGES:
ZONE OF ACCEPTANCE

Herbert Simon (1947) proposed that members of organizations (schools for example) vary in their need/desire to participate in decisions and in the implementation of decisions. This variation depends on whether or not a given decision falls into a staff member's *zone of acceptance*. Decisions that fall into this zone are those about which the member has little interest and from which the member perceives there will be little personal or work-related impact. On the other hand, those decisions that might impact the member and that are of interest to the member, are considered to be outside the zone of acceptance.

Edwin Bridges (1967) refers to the decisions in which the member has some stake as *relevant*. He proposes that, as the level of relevance to members increases, so will their desire to be included in the decision making and implementation process. However, the administrator's choices about involvement, asserts Bridges, should be based not only on the degree to which decisions are relevant, but also on the degree to which participants have some knowledge or expertise to contribute to the decision and its implementation.

Applying Simon's and Bridges' work, the administrator might draw these conclusions about delegating authority for decision making and for implementing decisions:

- ◆ As relevance increases, so should the administrator's propensity to include members in making and implementing decisions; however,

- ◆ The expertise of members is an important consideration; if they lack knowledge to contribute to the processes of making and implementing particular decisions, participation and authority should be limited.

- ◆ If the relevance of a decision/assignment to members is limited, but they have expertise to contribute, their participation, on a limited basis, is appropriate.

♦ When both relevance and expertise are absent, participation by members in either decision making or implementation is usually not warranted.

These guiding propositions for applying these theories to the real world of practice can be placed on a continuum, as demonstrated in Figure 3.2.

FIGURE 3.2. PARTICIPATION LEVELS FOR MEMBERS BASED ON ZONES OF ACCEPTANCE, RELEVANCE, AND DEGREE OF EXPERTISE

	No Participation	*Controlled, Limited, or Structured Participation*	*High Participation*
	◄———————————————————————————►		
Simon:	Inside zone of acceptance		Outside zone of acceptance
Bridges:	Issue irrelevant to member		Issue relevant to member
	Member has no expertise		Member has much expertise

This continuum is anchored by the level of participation, with none on one end, full participation on the other, and controlled or limited participation in the center. The center zone reflects circumstances in which the degree to which the decision falls within the zone of acceptance is partial, or in which the degree of relevance or expertise for members is only moderate. The center zone might also reflect circumstances in which either relevance or expertise are present, but not both.

EXPANDING THE MODEL: VROOM AND YETTON'S RULES FOR MEMBER INVOLVEMENT

Victor Vroom and Phillip Yetton (1973) proposed a useful, although somewhat complex, model for member involvement in decision making and delegation. The model describes different decision-making circumstances and prescribes appropriate leader behavior and levels of member involvement for each situation (refer to the levels of participation illustrated in Figure 3.1, p. 24).

Vroom and Yetton's prescriptions for leader behavior and member involvement are offered in the form of two sets of rules. The first set of rules is intended to improve the *quality* of decisions. Hoy and Miskel (1991) describe these quality rules as:

♦ The information rule: If the quality of the decision is important and if the leader does not possess sufficient information and expertise to solve the problem alone, then a unilateral decision is inappropriate; in fact, its use risks a low-quality decision.

♦ The trust rule: If the quality of the decisions is important and if the members cannot be trusted to decide on the basis of the organizational goals, then decision through group consensus is inappropriate. Indeed, the leader's lack of control over the decision may jeopardize its quality.

♦ The unstructured problem rule: Given an important decision, if the leader lacks information or expertise and if the problem is unstructured, then the method chosen to solve the problem should include sufficient procedures for collecting information. Participation of knowledgeable members should improve the quality of the decision.

The second set of rules, designed to improve *acceptance* of decisions by organization members, is described by Hoy and Miskel as:

♦ The acceptance rule: If subordinate acceptance of the decision is critical for effective implementation and if it is not certain that an autocratic decision would be accepted, then some sharing of the situation and participation of others are necessary. To deny any participation in the decision making risks the necessary acceptance.

- ◆ The conflict rule: If acceptance of the decision is critical and if an autocratic decision is not certain to be accepted, then the decision-making process should be structured to enable those in disagreement to resolve their differences with full knowledge of the problem. Thus, group participation is necessary; all members should have an opportunity to resolve any differences.

- ◆ The fairness rule: If the quality of the decision is not important, but its acceptance is critical and problematic, then a group decision should be made. A group decision will likely generate more acceptance and commitment than a hierarchical one.

- ◆ The acceptance priority rule: If acceptance is critical, not assured by an autocratic decision, and if members can be trusted, only group decision making is appropriate. Any other method provides the unnecessary risk that the decision will not be fully accepted nor receive the necessary subordinate commitment.

These guiding propositions for applying these rule sets to the real world of practice can also be placed on a continuum, as demonstrated in Figure 3.3.

Vroom and Yetton's model contributes new information and augments the work of Simon and Bridges. These theories provide school leaders with an expanded list of factors to consider when deciding whether to delegate decisions and how to do so.

EXPLODING THE MODEL: HERSEY AND BLANCHARD'S SITUATIONAL LEADERSHIP THEORY

To this point, we have developed a shared and basic understanding of how selected theories have helped to identify some of the factors administrators consider in deciding when to delegate. We now integrate this information with additional theories that provide insight into how leaders behave under these different modes of delegation.

FIGURE 3.3. PARTICIPATION LEVELS FOR MEMBERS BASED ON THE QUALITY AND ACCEPTANCE NEEDED FOR THE DECISION (ADAPTED FROM VROOM AND YETTON)

	No Participation	*Controlled, Limited, or Structured Participation*	*High Participation*
Rule Set One	Leader information sufficient — Structured problem		Leader information insufficient — Unstructured problem
Rule Set Two	Member acceptance not critical for implementation — Low probability of conflict — Member commitment not essential	High probability of conflict	Member acceptance critical for implementation — Conflicts can be effectively resolved by group — Member commitment essential

Paul Hersey and Kenneth Blanchard (1977, 1982) are the primary authors associated with the notion of situational leadership. Central to the model is the assumption that leader behavior will vary according to situational circumstances. Primary among these circumstances is the maturity of members in the organization. Maturity in this context refers to *task maturity*, a construct that is different from the behavioral attributes one would ordinarily associate with the term. Hersey and Blanchard define task maturity as the experience, knowledge, skills, willingness to accept responsibility, and goal-setting ability of the individual or group (1982). The model, as adapted in Figure 3.4, describes four types of leadership behavior, which can vary depending on the task maturity of the individual or group.

It is important to note that task maturity is situation specific. In other words, the level of maturity can vary within the same individual or group depending on the task at hand. Individuals or groups who possess a high level of maturity in one circumstance, may be considerably less mature when confronted with a new assignment or a novel decision-making situation.

As a case in point, consider the very capable classroom teacher who is asked to become a member of an interview team that will participate in the screening of applicants for a vacant assistant principal's position. While this individual is clearly mature with respect to the task of teaching a class, the teacher may lack expertise in the specific criteria by which applicants for an assistant principalship should be judged. This teacher may have only scant knowledge of the personnel laws that govern the conduct of such interviews. The teacher may even be only marginally interested in the process. The challenge for the school administrator is to recognize and respond appropriately to such variances in task maturity.

Note the similarity between the concept of task maturity and Bridges' concept of expertise. The absence or presence of task maturity could easily be substituted for the absence or presence of expertise in the continuum at the bottom of Figure 3.2 (p. 26). It is important to recognize, however, that Hersey and Blanchard made an explicit case that such a judgment should be situationally based. That is, staff levels of task maturity or expertise may vary from one situation to another such that different levels of participation are appropriate for different decisions. As an illustration, return to the example of the teacher who is asked to participate in the interview team. The leader may determine that, based on the task maturity of the individual, it is more appropriate for the teacher to assist in screening résumés and applications, but not in the interview process or final selection decision. This might qualify as Level 2 participation in the hierarchy outlined in Figure 3.1 (p. 24).

Building on Ohio State University leadership studies (Hemphill & Koons, 1950; Halpin, 1966), which classified leader behaviors as either initiating structure (emphasizing productivity) or initiating consideration (emphasizing interpersonal domains), Hersey and Blanchard (1982) assigned leadership styles

FIGURE 3.4. LEADER BEHAVIOR, TASK MATURITY MATRIX (ADAPTED FROM BLAKE & MOUTON, 1985, AND HERSEY & BLANCHARD, 1982)

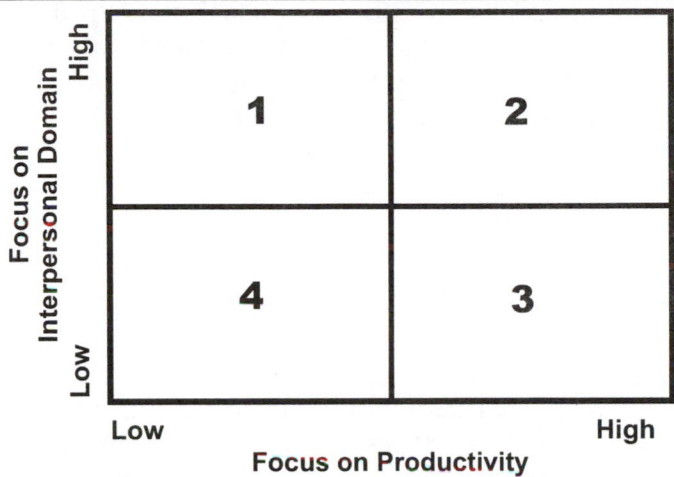

Quadrant 1: Low productivity/high interpersonal emphasis on the part of the leader. Appropriate for participants with moderate to high levels of maturity for the task at hand. Such individuals can be assigned decisions and tasks with minimal oversight by the leader, but have some need for encouragement and interaction (see Figure 3.1, p. 24, Levels 2 and 3).

Quadrant 2: Leader demonstrates high productivity/high interpersonal emphasis. Appropriate for participants with low to moderate levels of maturity for the task at hand. The leader is likely to control, limit, or structure the participation of such individuals, and is likely to follow up, encourage, and interact with them more frequently (see Figure 3.1, p. 24 , Levels 2 and 3).

Quadrant 3: High productivity/low interpersonal emphasis on the part of the leader. Appropriate for participants with low levels of maturity for the task at hand. The leader is less likely to delegate tasks and decisions to such individuals (see Figure 3.1, p. 24, Level 1).

Quadrant 4: Low productivity/low interpersonal behaviors. Appropriate for participants with high levels of maturity for the task at hand. Such individuals can be assigned decisions and tasks with little need for subsequent involvement on the part of the leader (see Figure 3.1, p. 24, Level 4).

to the continuum we have used in Figures 3.1 (p. 24), 3.2 (p. 26), and 3.3 (p. 29) to visualize appropriate levels of participation. They contended that the four leader styles of behavior (Figure 3.4) were directly related to the level of task maturity of the individual or group with whom the administrator was concerned. Furthermore, the styles could be recognized by the degree of emphasis the leader placed on getting the task accomplished through relationships with people. Thus, Figures 3.2 and 3.3 might be revised to give insight into specific leadership behaviors appropriate for the delegation factors discussed.

Figure 3.5 illustrates the integration of Hersey and Blanchard's leadership behavior styles with the constructs developed in Figures 3.2 and 3.3.

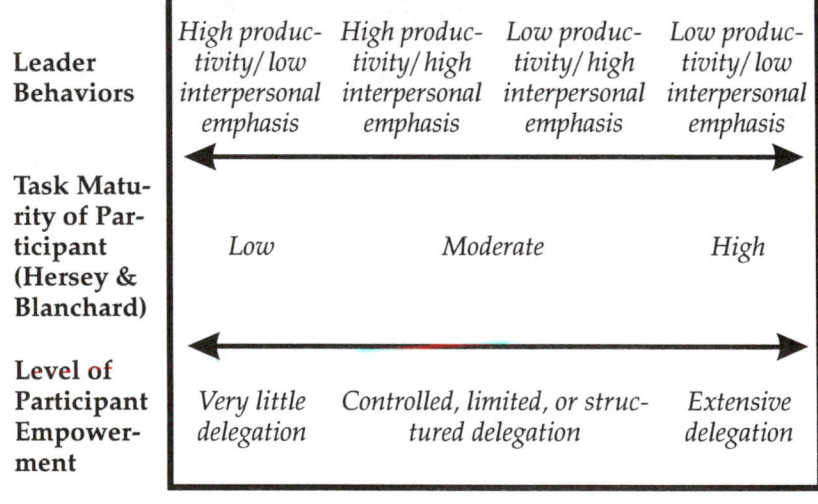

FIGURE 3.5. INTERACTION BETWEEN LEADER STYLE AND LEVELS OF EMPOWERMENT BASED ON ZONES OF ACCEPTANCE, RELEVANCE, DEGREE OF EXPERTISE, TASK MATURITY, AND QUALITY OF DECISION (SEE FIGURES 3.2, p. 26, 3.3, p. 29, & 3.4, p. 31)

Leader Behaviors	*High productivity/low interpersonal emphasis*	*High productivity/high interpersonal emphasis*	*Low productivity/high interpersonal emphasis*	*Low productivity/low interpersonal emphasis*
Task Maturity of Participant (Hersey & Blanchard)	*Low*	*Moderate*		*High*
Level of Participant Empowerment	*Very little delegation*	*Controlled, limited, or structured delegation*		*Extensive delegation*

WHICH CONTINGENCIES AFFECT DELEGATION AND EMPOWERMENT?

This chapter has introduced several prominent theoretical models in order to develop a framework for understanding and acting on some of the factors administrators consider as they decide whether or not to delegate. This framework was integrated with theories of leadership to illustrate how administrators who are using different modes of delegation behave in their leadership activities. Blending such information effectively provides administrators with tools to enhance performance, motivation, and satisfaction of staff members.

Subsequent chapters introduce an even wider array of theories that inform the process of delegation. While each theory is certainly instructive on its own, it is worthwhile to glean from such models a comprehensive list of variables, or contingencies, which the prudent administrator will want to consider as he or she practices the important skill of delegation. The models discussed in this chapter, and a preview of additional models, reveal six categories of delegation contingencies:

- ◆ Leader Contingencies: those characteristics of leaders in the organization that impact decision making and delegation;

- ◆ Task Contingencies: the nature of the role, responsibility, or function that is the focus of decision making and/or delegation;

- ◆ Member Contingencies: those attributes of school staff members and stakeholders that are critical to effective decision making and delegation;

- ◆ Group Contingencies: the collective characteristics of groups of members; these characteristics are unique to groups and are not simply the sum of individual attributes;

- ◆ Resource Contingencies: the funding, equipment, space, time, and so on, that are needed or perceived to be needed by persons in fulfilling delegated tasks;

- ◆ Authority Contingencies: those jurisdictional considerations (laws, regulations, policies) that may constrain the discretion of persons involved in decision making and delegation.

The next several chapters explore these delegation contingencies in detail. In addition, the implications of these contingencies for administrative effectiveness are analyzed. Finally, strategies for effective leadership behavior related to delegation are suggested.

APPLYING YOUR KNOWLEDGE

1. Consider the three lists that you constructed under "Your Thoughts Are?" at the beginning of this chapter.

   - First, examine your third list, those implicit factors Jan might be using as she decides what to delegate. Are any of these factors similar to the variables described in Simon and Bridges' theories? How are they similar? Why did you include them?

   - Now select two items from each of the first two lists of decisions Jan might delegate and might not delegate. Use Simon and Bridges' theories to evaluate whether each decision should stay on the list you made or be shifted to the other list. Explain why you retain or move each of the items.

   - On your lists, identify the decisions that might require controlled or limited participation? Why?

2. Using the information from Vroom and Yetton's "Rules for Member Involvement":

   - Repeat the first activity above, substituting the variables in the Vroom and Yetton model for those supplied by Simon and Bridges.

   - Applying the Vroom and Yetton model, repeat the second activity from above, using a different set of decisions from each of the first two lists of decisions that Jan might delegate and might not delegate.

- Repeat the final activity from above, using Vroom and Yetton's rules to identify decisions that might require controlled or limited participation.

3. Review the integrated theoretical model outlined in Figure 3.5 (p. 32). Consider the following potential delegation circumstances. Imagine yourself as the school's principal in each instance. Decide which, if any, members of the school staff or school community should be involved in the decision. Discuss how and why certain variables might cause you to reach different delegation decisions for each of the three circumstances.

   - It is time to prepare the master schedule for the middle school in which you serve as principal. This process includes assigning faculty to teams and to teaching assignments. Suggest a process that can be used to develop the master schedule.

   - You are the principal of the school district's only elementary school. The human sexuality curriculum that is taught in the fifth grade is seriously out of date and you have been placed in charge of this curriculum revision project. How will you carry out this assignment?

4. Interview practicing administrators about factors they consider when making various types of decisions and when delegating roles, responsibilities, and functions to others.

5. Interview teachers and/or community members regarding their perceptions of the nature of decisions and tasks that are delegated to them by school administrators. What do they perceive to be the factors that administrators consider when engaging in delegation?

4

LEADER CONTINGENCIES AND THEIR EFFECT ON DELEGATION

SETTING THE STAGE

THE SITUATION

These statements were made by different administrators who were undertaking staff development to learn about participative decision-making, empowerment, and collegiality:

- ◆ "We want these people to feel that they are involved in decision making here."
- ◆ "When I delegate a decision, I want to be sure the group will make the same decision I would."
- ◆ "We can't have any red shirts here; everyone has to participate in all the decisions."
- ◆ "Yes, I believe in delegation, but someone has to yank the chain around here."
- ◆ "Sure, I support employee involvement; but my job is on the line when the work isn't done properly."
- ◆ "I trust the group to accomplish the task in a way that will work best in our situation."
- ◆ "If I delegate this to a group and they don't do it right, what's going to happen when I change it so it is done the way it's supposed to be done?"

YOUR THOUGHTS ARE?

With your colleagues or classmates, or individually, reexamine these quotes to tentatively discern any underlying attributes of the administrators who made them. What do you think are their true perspectives about inclusive decision-making and delegation? What related skills do you suspect each may possess or lack? Compare notes with your colleagues in order to clarify and expand your own assumptions about the perspectives and skills of these administrators.

INTRODUCTION

Chapter 3 introduced a number of contingencies that influence decision making and delegation. Perhaps the most influential contingencies are the skills and dispositions of school leaders themselves. As the quotes in Setting the Stage indicate, leader attributes affect the propensity to include others and to delegate, as well as the manner in which leaders monitor and evaluate delegation outcomes. Awareness of these contingencies and the capacity to develop one's own leadership skills in the areas of decision making and delegation are important considerations for effective administration.

The following sections provide a brief review of selected literature about administrator traits and characteristics that can influence delegation strategies. Suggestions and guides are offered to school leaders as they consider the relationship of their own skills and attitudes to effective delegation.

LEADER CONTINGENCIES

ATTITUDINAL COMPONENT

School administrators report that the use of delegation is strongly related to managerial effectiveness. In fact, their assessments of the importance of delegation are similar to the assessments made by managers in other professions (Ordidge, 1985). Like leaders in other kinds of organizations, school administrators also differ in their attitudes about and approaches to the involvement of others in decision-making and decision implementation.

In spite of the acknowledged importance of delegation, not all school administrators use this skill capably. Effective use of delegation is most influenced by the school administrator's own dispositions toward the involvement of others. These dispositions make up the *attitudinal* attributes of a school leader's delegation abilities. Democratic leadership requires the willingness of the administrator to empower members of the school community, as well as the capacity to aid the group's decision making activities (Gastil, 1994).

Of the attitudinal attributes, the administrator's own *self-concept* may be the greatest determinant of effective delegation. School leaders with high self-esteem are frequently more effective as delegators (Armenta & Reno, 1991). Perhaps they are more comfortable admitting a lack of knowledge and skills. In a study of principals in five states, King and Kerchner (1991) found that principals who effectively empower others feel free to admit deficiencies and to give up tasks/roles in which they see themselves as less skilled. Such individuals seem less concerned about appearing to be in charge than they are about using the best means possible to achieve organizational aims. Insecurities on the part of the administrator may impair their inclination to trust others and to relinquish decisions and tasks for fear of being outperformed by a subordinate.

Other personality traits impact an administrator's willingness and ability to delegate. Persons possessing a strong belief in *equality* may be more likely to delegate authority than those less disposed toward equality (Gray, O'Connor, & Decatur, 1994). Leader *optimism* and *honesty* are traits that tend to generate greater satisfaction and willingness to carry out assignments among teachers (Blase & Kirby, 1992).

Supportive, collaborative behavior on the part of the leader strengthens member satisfaction (Finch, 1977; Abdel-Halim, 1983) and performance (Abdel-Halim, 1983). *Nonpunitive* behavior and *minimizing subordinate fear* can also increase member creativity and satisfaction (Fulk & Wendler, 1982; Deming, 1986).

Member satisfaction does not automatically translate into better performance (Finch, 1977). In Chapter 3, we noted that more autocratic, directive, task-oriented leader behavior is sometimes in order, particularly when members or groups are less experienced, skilled, and motivated (Hersey & Blanchard, 1982; Blase & Kirby, 1992), or when tasks lack clarity (Mayes & Barton, 1987; Fulk & Wendler, 1982). However, the leader who is inordinately disposed toward directive behavior will learn that more mature and capable staff members find such behavior unacceptable (Hersey & Blanchard, 1982; Blase & Kirby, 1992). In team settings, *autocratic and controlling behaviors* will tend to stifle the creativity of the group, limit proposals from members, and risk bad decisions (Janis, 1982; Leana, 1985).

ABILITIES COMPONENT

Aside from personal attributes, there are certain leader *abilities* that are strongly related to effective delegation. If these attributes are viewed as abilities, they are more readily subject to change than attitudes and habits.

A key attribute of a leader who effectively includes others in decision making and decision implementation is the *management of the leader's own behavior* in group situations. Such behavior can range from highly directive to encouraging to altogether nonintrusive (Carew, Parisi-Carew, & Blanchard, 1986). While some teams may require greater assistance and direction than others, it is frequently observed that administrators who speak first in group decision-making settings, or who announce their predispositions toward decisions or plans, have an inhibiting effect on the creativity and participation of members.

The *conceptual complexity* of an administrator seems to influence how well that administrator is able to differentiate, discriminate, and integrate information—all of which are essential critical thinking abilities used in decision making, problem solving, and communication about delegation. The leader's level of critical thinking within these tasks is affected by the rate, load, and diversity of information that the leader can process in interpersonal interactions (Schroder, Driver, & Streufert, 1967). Clearly, participative decision-making and the inclusion of others in task completion increase the rate, load, and diversity of information. It is equally clear that processing such information demands administrators with high levels of conceptual complexity. In fact, numerous authors have observed that effective delegation requires administrators who are skilled in assessing the experience, talents, and motivation of others (Hersey & Blanchard, 1982; Wofford & Srinivasan, 1983; McCall, 1994).

Confidence in the intentions and abilities of subordinates is a key consideration in the process of delegation. Research suggests that school administrators tend, more than managers in other professions, to place greater confidence in the decision-making ability, organizational ability, and persistence of staff members (Ordidge, 1985). This may be because the school leader believes that teachers are typically very knowledgeable about the organization's primary goals—teaching, learning, and managing student behavior. Most delegated tasks are likely to revolve around these central purposes, thus affording the leader greater confidence in staff abilities to carry out these tasks.

An effective leader is able to *clarify the tasks and identify the parameters* (policies, laws, and decision-making constraints) within which individuals and groups need to operate (Wofford & Srinivasan, 1983; Mayes & Barton, 1987; Taylor & Card, 1985). House (1971) proposes a *path-goal theory* which, like Hersey and Blanchard's follower-based theory, suggests that decisions about participation and delegation should occur within the context of the particular situation. The *Path* refers to the means by which work *goals* are attained. According to the model leader behavior can increase member rewards for achieving work goals by clarifying the means or path to task completion, removing barriers, and enhancing member satisfaction in the process. Research shows that staff members whose leaders clarify their roles perform at higher levels than staff members for whom roles are inadequately clarified (Wofford & Srinivasan, 1983).

Finally, *clarifying parameters* is an important leader ability. Such parameters include identifying who is responsible for given tasks, what resources will be available, the time lines expected, and the decision-making discretion of the delegatees. Few circumstances will more seriously undermine an administrator's credibility and the trust of staff/community members than those in which the administrator fails to deliver on commitments of time and resources, reduces the decision-making authority of delegatees after the fact, or rejects the work and/or decisions of delegatees who originally perceived that they had broad discretion.

It appears evident that leader attributes are contingencies which significantly affect both the willingness of school administrators to delegate and the effectiveness of such delegation. A summary of the leader attributes that the literature suggests are most closely associated with effectiveness in this important administrative role is presented in Figure 4.1.

FIGURE 4.1. SUMMARY OF LEADER CONTINGENCIES THAT AFFECT DELEGATION

Attitudinal Traits
- Self-concept
- Orientation toward equality
- Optimism
- Honesty
- Orientation toward supportive collaborative relationships
- Orientation toward directive leadership and productivity
- Orientation toward intimidation and punishment
- Group interaction propensities

Ability Traits
- Self-management in team situations
- Conceptual complexity
- Ability to assess the capacity of others
- Trust/confidence in others
- Ability to clarify tasks and parameters

LEADER TRAITS: IMPROVING THE PERSONAL CAPACITY FOR EFFECTIVE DELEGATION

The previous sections of this chapter identify leader contingencies related to effective of delegation. Knowledge of these contingencies is useful, but only if the administrator thoughtfully analyzes his or her own attitudes and abilities. The following sections are a guide to such an analysis and to improving one's capacity for effective delegation.

KNOW THYSELF

Surely no other contingency domain is more critical to successful delegation than the leader's own attitudes and abilities.

For this reason, self-awareness and the ability to critically examine one's own strengths and weaknesses for delegation are extremely important. There are a number of ways to self-assess, but these activities are valuable only if the administrator is willing to use the results for professional improvement.

A number of instruments are available to assist in assessing leader attitudes and abilities. However, some may wish to approach such assessment less formally. Figure 4.2 is an informal self-assessment, which lists a number of statements related to leader dispositions associated with effective delegation. Complete the assessment and consider the implications of your responses as indicators of your potential effectiveness in delegating. Give additional thought to how you might grow in those areas where your responses fell disproportionately into the "as often as not," "occasionally," or "never" ranges.

SELF-APPRAISAL AS A GUIDE TO DELEGATION

Although this text is useful to a number of school and other leaders, it is primarily instructive to principals and prospective principals. Analyzing the roles of the principal and one's own strengths in relationship to these roles is important for such individuals. Figure 4.3 (pp. 45–47) outlines North Carolina's 10 performance domains for the principal, that have been developed through a comprehensive and inclusive process (Ward, 1996).

Use these performance domains as a guide to self-appraisal. Determine areas in which you will wish to strengthen your skills, and areas in which you may wish to employ the strengths of others in order to complement your own deficiencies.

Develop a plan for strengthening your competence in areas where you perceive both a deficiency and the need to be directly involved in managing this area of responsibility. Consider the degree to which you believe that responsibilities in some domains might appropriately be delegated in order to capitalize on the strengths of others. Who would such persons be? What skills would they possess?

FIGURE 4.2. KNOW THYSELF:
A LEADER'S SELF-ASSESSMENT

As a self-assessment tool, consider the extent to which you agree with each of the following statements. Rate yourself according to this continuum: Always— Usually—As Often As Not—Occasionally—Never

◆ Self-concept
  • I feel successful in my work.
  • I recognize my own strengths and weaknesses.
  • I am committed to my work.
  • I encourage the personal development of others.
  • I acknowledge the contributions of others to the success of the school.

◆ Equality
  • I actively seek out diverse perspectives/ideas.
  • I value others' perspectives/ideas.
  • I involve others in decision making.
  • I have support and respect for my colleagues.

◆ Optimism
  • I have confidence in the words and actions of others.
  • People are dependable and reliable.
  • People can be trusted to handle details.
  • I feel people are committed to their work.

◆ Honesty
  • I fairly represent the work involved in projects.
  • I share relevant information openly with others.
  • I clarify work expectations and outcomes.
  • I seek to resolve misunderstandings.

FIGURE 4.3. NORTH CAROLINA'S PERFORMANCE DOMAINS FOR PRINCIPALS

The following table contains ten role clusters or areas of expertise relevant to the role of school principal. First, appraise your level of comfort in each role by checking one of the three boxes in the second column (i.e., Appraisal of Self in Role). Next, indicate your desire to become more comfortable in the role by checking the appropriate box in the third column (i.e., Desire to Learn the Role). The resulting profile will help you to determine which roles you may wish to focus on in your professional development and which responsibilities you may wish to delegate. Write a plan of action including strategies to become more comfortable in the role(s) you wish to improve.

Role Clusters	Appraisal of Self in Role	Desire to Learn the Role	Plan of Action for Professional Development	Persons to Whom Significant Responsibility in this Area can be Delegated
A. Facilitates the development, implementation, and communication of a shared school vision	☐ Very Comfortable ☐ Comfortable ☐ Uncomfortable	☐ High Desire ☐ Moderate Desire ☐ Low Desire	_____ _____ _____ _____ _____	(1) _____ (2) _____ (3) _____
B. Promotes the development of organizational, instructional, and assessment strategies to enhance teaching and learning	☐ Very Comfortable ☐ Comfortable ☐ Uncomfortable	☐ High Desire ☐ Moderate Desire ☐ Low Desire	_____ _____ _____ _____ _____	(1) _____ (2) _____ (3) _____
C. Works with others to insure a working and learning climate that is safe, secure, and respectful of diversity	☐ Very Comfortable ☐ Comfortable ☐ Uncomfortable	☐ High Desire ☐ Moderate Desire ☐ Low Desire	_____ _____ _____ _____ _____	(1) _____ (2) _____ (3) _____

(Continued)

Role Clusters	Appraisal of Self in Role	Desire to Learn the Role	Plan of Action for Professional Development	Persons to Whom Significant Responsibility in this Area can be Delegated
D. Demonstrates integrity and behaves in an ethical manner	☐ Very Comfortable ☐ Comfortable ☐ Uncomfortable	☐ High Desire ☐ Moderate Desire ☐ Low Desire	_____	(1) _____ (2) _____ (3) _____
E. Facilitates school improvement by engaging the school community's stakeholders in collaboration, problem solving, and shared decision-making	☐ Very Comfortable ☐ Comfortable ☐ Uncomfortable	☐ High Desire ☐ Moderate Desire ☐ Low Desire	_____	(1) _____ (2) _____ (3) _____
F. Uses excellent management and leadership skills to achieve effective and efficient organizational operations	☐ Very Comfortable ☐ Comfortable ☐ Uncomfortable	☐ High Desire ☐ Moderate Desire ☐ Low Desire	_____	(1) _____ (2) _____ (3) _____
G. Employs effective interpersonal, communication, and public relations skills	☐ Very Comfortable ☐ Comfortable ☐ Uncomfortable	☐ High Desire ☐ Moderate Desire ☐ Low Desire	_____	(1) _____ (2) _____ (3) _____

(Continued)

Role Clusters	Appraisal of Self in Role	Desire to Learn the Role	Plan of Action for Professional Development	Persons to Whom Significant Responsibility in this Area can be Delegated
H. Demonstrates academic success, intellectual ability, and a commitment to life-long learning	☐ Very Comfortable ☐ Comfortable ☐ Uncomfortable	☐ High Desire ☐ Moderate Desire ☐ Low Desire	_____ _____ _____ _____	(1) _____ (2) _____ (3) _____
I. Promotes the appropriate use of valid and reliable information to facilitate progress, evaluate personnel and programs, and to make decisions	☐ Very Comfortable ☐ Comfortable ☐ Uncomfortable	☐ High Desire ☐ Moderate Desire ☐ Low Desire	_____ _____ _____ _____	(1) _____ (2) _____ (3) _____
J. Fosters a culture of continuous improvement focused upon teaching and learning	☐ Very Comfortable ☐ Comfortable ☐ Uncomfortable	☐ High Desire ☐ Moderate Desire ☐ Low Desire	_____ _____ _____ _____	(1) _____ (2) _____ (3) _____

GUIDES FOR LEADER PARTICIPATION IN GROUPS

As shared decision making, school-based governance, and total quality management become more common in school leadership, skill in working with groups will be essential for principals and other school leaders. In working with teams to make and implement decisions, leaders must consider the impact of their own behavior on group dynamics.

Naturally, some teams require greater assistance and direction from a leader than others. However, as was noted earlier, more directive leader behaviors can have an inhibiting effect on team processes. It is important, therefore, for the school leader to recognize his or her tendencies in this important management domain as the first step toward maximizing the potential of team decision-making and task completion.

The assessment in Figure 4.4 provides an opportunity for you to examine your behavior in work groups. The assessment is grounded on two assumptions. First, that members are capable and knowledgeable with regard to the decision or task to be addressed. Second, that the descriptors on the right side of the scale are the more desirable leader behaviors for groups. Respond to the items honestly, and if the analysis suggests that you tend toward dominant leadership behavior in groups, consider the reasons. More importantly, consider the circumstances and/or professional growth that might encourage you toward a more facilitative style of leadership.

This section and the assessment in Figure 4.4 introduced the topics related to group contingencies in the process of delegation. These topics are explored in greater detail in Chapter 7.

SUMMARY

This chapter introduced important leader traits and abilities as contingencies that affect the processes of delegation and empowerment. Honest self-appraisal is critical to an administrator's growth and effectiveness in these areas. The assessments outlined, along with the exercises in the following section, should be useful for gaining insight into one's own dispositions and abilities and for suggesting potential avenues for personal and professional growth.

FIGURE 4.4. SELF-ASSESSMENT:
LEADER PARTICIPATION IN GROUPS

As another self-assessment, consider the bipolar descriptors on the semantic differential scales below. Place a checkmark nearest the adjective or phrase that most closely describes your behavior in group settings.

Dominating ⟵——————————⟶ *Collaborating*

Initiates	___:___:___:___:___:___:___ Facilitates
Tells Ideas	___:___:___:___:___:___:___ Inspires Ideas
Own Goals	___:___:___:___:___:___:___ Mutual Goals
Defines	___:___:___:___:___:___:___ Empowers
Persuades	___:___:___:___:___:___:___ Attends/Listens

APPLYING YOUR KNOWLEDGE

1. Check your original hunches

   Return to the lists that you made in response to "Setting the Stage" at the beginning of this chapter. How does your list compare with those identified in the Figure 4.1 (p. 42)? Which of the attributes on your list and on the list in Figure 4.1 are most helpful to you in analyzing the relationship between leader contingencies and effective delegation?

2. Know Thyself…Through the Eyes of Others

   Using the scales in the self-assessments in Figures 4.2 (p. 44) and 4.4 (p. 49), ask a trusted colleague who knows you well to rate you according to the assessment items. If you want to gain additional insight into how you are perceived, ask a group of people with whom you work, preferably colleagues or subordinates, to anonymously assess you using these instruments. Consider the implications of the responses for your own professional growth.

3. Use your knowledge

   With colleagues or classmates, develop three or four scenarios that offer an administrator the opportunity to delegate a decision or task (e.g., scheduling, hiring new personnel, or developing a new curriculum). Be sure that the scenarios differ in the level of risk to the administrator. Identify three or four administrators whom you believe differ on some of the leadership traits described in this chapter. Interview the administrators and ask them what level of delegation they would employ with their current staff for each of the scenarios; you may want to differentiate levels of delegation according to the descriptions in Figure 3.1 (p. 24). Analyze your findings to see which of the leader traits described in this chapter apply to each administrator. Which administrator(s) do you predict is the most effective at delegation and empowerment? Why?

4. Expand your knowledge

Search the literature for these concepts: locus of control; authoritarianism; self-concept; fear of failure; dogmatism. There may be other topics that arise out of this reading. Look for information that helps you understand:

- How the concept influences leader behavior in the areas of delegation and empowerment.

- How a person might improve his or her level of leadership behavior if needed.

5. Develop a personal improvement plan

Using the information about yourself that you've gleaned from the self-assessments in the chapter, prepare a personal improvement plan. The plan should specify those leader attributes that you want to improve, your strategies for making the improvements (including reading and staff development), your timetable for the improvements, and strategies you'll use to evaluate how real and significant your improvements are.

5

TASK CONTINGENCIES AND THEIR EFFECT ON DELEGATION

SETTING THE STAGE

THE SITUATION

Principal Bill Amato drives to the office on Saturday morning to have some quiet time to catch up on his work. He retrieves the personal "to do" list that he's been compiling. The list, in no particular order of priority, includes the following:

- Work on curriculum for a two-year Algebra program for students who are less proficient in math
- Resolve schedule dispute arising from use of the tennis courts by school and community groups
- Assess building maintenance and repair needs for the coming year's budget requests
- Handle neighborhood homeowners' complaints about students dropping trash on streets and lawns en route to and from school
- Generate ideas for a grant proposal to support the creation of an alternative program for chronically disruptive students
- Develop proposed evaluation criteria and portfolio process for a revised teacher performance appraisal system
- Replace P. A. system on the football field

- Per the superintendent's request, prepare a response to parent complaints, made at the last school board meeting, that the school is placing "social promotion" ahead of academic criteria in advancing students through the grade levels
- Develop plan for designing and implementing a character education program in the school

YOUR THOUGHTS ARE?

Within small teams, carefully consider how these tasks are different from or similar to each other. Be as specific as possible in selecting single words or short phrases that adequately capture differences or similarities in these tasks, and explain your rationale. Share your team's work with other groups and develop a composite list of ways you can classify or analyze these tasks.

Identify some of the other items that you might find on an administrator's "to do" list and assess the degree to which your composite list of adjectives is complete. If you need to add more words or phrases, do so. Now, assuming the validity of each classification generated, how would you expect these differences to influence administrative delegation and why?

INTRODUCTION

Chapter 3 introduced selected contingencies, drawn from formal theoretical models, which affect an administrator's determinations about participative decision-making and delegation. Chapter 4 expanded the list of delegation contingencies to include selected administrator attributes. As your work in the Setting the Stage activities suggests, the nature of the decision/task/responsibility is another important contingency in effective delegation.

Tasks and decisions that an administrator may delegate are numerous, and all tasks are not alike. As a result of this, scholars have attempted to identify differences associated with various types of tasks. A primary reason for doing so is to better match the task and the employee for optimum productivity. Thus, differences in tasks are key matters that must be considered by an administrator if the administrator is to be effective in matters of shared decision-making and delegation.

This chapter offers a brief overview of relevant literature on task contingencies affecting delegation. Suggestions are given to guide school leaders as they factor task variation into plans for delegation.

SELECTED TASK CONTINGENCIES AND DELEGATION

For clarity, delegation and participation contingencies are divided into two classes. The first class consists of those arising from the task itself; the second class consists of those resulting from the interactions between a task and the individual who is assigned to the task.

THE NATURE OF THE TASK

In administrative literature, work tasks and decisions are described in numerous ways. Early contributors, such as Simon (1947) and Drucker (1954), classified tasks and decisions as:

- Routine or novel
- Well-defined or ill-defined
- Programmable or nonprogrammable
- Fact or value based
- Structured or unstructured

Each of the first descriptors in the adjective pair reflects a task or decision for which there is a *knowable best* solution and a finite group of strategies for arriving at that solution. The second set of descriptors reflect tasks and decisions for which there are many *possible best* solutions and many ways of determining which solution or decision will prevail. To acquire more understanding of these differences, take a few minutes to discuss with your colleagues or classmates which adjective in the pairs above best describes each of these tasks or decisions:

- Deciding the most efficient bus route.
- Selecting the most appropriate reading text.
- Deciding what time of day to schedule a Physics class so that the most students who need it can get in

it with the fewest numbers of conflicts with other classes.

♦ Deciding on a revised mission for the school.

♦ Deciding whether to use a traditional or a block schedule.

♦ Selecting a teacher evaluation instrument.

♦ Developing a citizenship education program.

Clearly, the second and fourth through seventh tasks are different than the first and third tasks. The latter would most appropriately be characterized by descriptors such as routine, programmable, and structured, while the former would better fit the second word in each set of task descriptors.

Research indicates that more complex, novel, unstructured, nonprogrammable tasks are completed with a higher degree of accuracy when undertaken by a group (Sousa, 1982). Others have found that when the task or decision requires a high level of quality, groups are more effective than individuals (Conway, 1984; Vroom, 1964).

Tasks have been classified in other ways. Hackman and Oldham (1975) differentiate tasks according to the clarity of the task, the skills needed for completion of the task, the significance of the task, and the level of authority, and feedback associated with the task. Tasks are also classified according to the level of stimulation they provide, the degree to which they are repetitive, inspection, or continuous control tasks, and the extent to which they require specific skills such as identification, discrimination, sequencing, scanning, or problem solving (Fisher, 1993; Fleishman, 1978).

To further illustrate these classifications, consider the following. *Identification tasks* (e.g., developing a list of all students in the school receiving free and reduced-cost lunches) are clearly different than *discrimination tasks* (e.g., discerning whether one student's statements are more credible than the statements of another). Both of these can be differentiated from *sequencing tasks* (e.g., scheduling students so that all those taking single-section courses can be enrolled in the courses they've selected) and *problem-solving tasks* (e.g., determining why so many students are failing Algebra I). Such tasks vary in the amount of *repetition, continuous control,* and *inspection* that they require. This emerging field of work urges administrators to seek greater specificity in assessing the nature and implicit demands of a task.

We can assume that identification and sequencing tasks are less complex mental operations than are discriminating and problem-solving tasks. Further, repetitive tasks would seem to be more routine and structured, whereas inspection and continuous control tasks would seem to be more novel and less structured.

Some psychologists analyze the nature of a task on the basis of the degree of risk inherent in the task (Bem, Wallach, & Kogan, 1963; Burstein & Vinokur, 1975; Stoner, 1961). The discussion of risks associated with a decision or task is particularly important for schools, where the environment often does not support risk taking (Murphy, 1994b). Norms are often deeply entrenched, and communities are sometimes skeptical of experimentation in schools, especially when students are perceived to be the *guinea pigs*.

Groups are more likely to accept higher risks than are individuals (Stoner, 1961). A task fraught with social risk, such as developing a required health curriculum on AIDS, clearly should not be delegated to one school staff member or to a group that is inexperienced and unskilled in the political and technical aspects of curriculum development. Tasks associated with highly controversial issues are more appropriate for groups (preferably task-mature groups) than for individuals. Reassurance from the leader is important with high-risk tasks. Deming, in his principles of total quality management, maintains that a leader has an obligation to drive out fear, especially in high-risk situations, because of the negative impact it has on communication and progress (Walton, 1986).

Other psychologists analyze the task in terms of its dimensionality (Dykes & Cooper, 1978). In general, they report that tasks with integral or separable dimensions are approached differently and that different people require different amounts of time for processing them. Tasks with inseparable dimensions would seem to be more complex, requiring, if not higher-order mental processes, at least multiple information-processing perspectives.

Holistic and analytic styles for processing information are not distributed equally among the population, and style does influence the quality and speed of solutions (Dykes & Cooper, 1978). This suggests that complex tasks having multiple dimensions are more appropriate for groups than individuals, if for no other reason than to insure the capacities needed to fully analyze the problem.

Clearly, the nature of tasks is an important contingency in delegation. The nature of the task presents administrators with another guide for selecting an appropriate level of participation in decision making and delegation. Using a format similar to that used in Figures 3.2 (p. 26), 3.3 (p. 29), and 3.5 (p. 32), this material can be applied and summarized as in the participation-delegation model in Figure 5.1.

FIGURE 5.1. PARTICIPATION LEVELS FOR MEMBERS BASED ON THE NATURE OF THE TASK

	Low Participation & Delegation	*Controlled, Limited or Structured Participation & Delegation*	*High Participation & Delegation*
Simon, Drucker	Routine Well-structured Fact based		Novel Ill-structured Value based
Fleishman, Fisher	Repetitive Identification Sequencing		Inspection Continuous control Discrimination Problem solving
Stone	Low risk		High risk
Dykes, Cooper	Separable dimensions		Inseparable dimensions

APPLYING THE MODEL TO PRACTICE

Return to Bill's "to do list" in "Your Thoughts Please." Divide the list among teams of your classmates or groups of your colleagues. Use the information presented as a basis for task analysis. Make a list of the task adjectives presented in this section which most apply to item(s) from the list that your team was assigned.

Using the model in Figure 5.1, discuss the optimum level of participation or delegation implicit in the items your group was assigned. Discuss your decisions and rationale with your class mates.

INTERACTIONS BETWEEN TASKS AND INDIVIDUALS

It is necessary, but insufficient, to analyze the task alone as a basis for selecting appropriate levels of participation or forms of delegation. In other words, administrators cannot delegate effectively on the basis of task characteristics alone. The reason lies in the interaction between people and the work that they do. This has been the driving force in other analyses of work in organizations such as schools. Effective participation and delegation strategies must be based on a simultaneous assessment of the relationship between task and the persons who will be involved with the task (Fisher, 1993).

For example, House (1971) proposes a *path-goal* theory that, like Hersey and Blanchard's model, bases prescriptions for leader behavior in delegating decisions and tasks on the context of the particular situation and the nature of the particular task. *Path* refers to the means by which work *goals* are attained. Embedded within the model is the notion that leader behavior can increase member prospects for achieving work goals by clarifying the means or path to goal attainment, by removing barriers, and by enhancing member satisfaction in the process.

When these propositions are operationalized as prescriptions for leader behavior, House suggested that:

- In circumstances where the task or role is novel and/or complex, directive behavior on the part of the leader will increase member motivation and satisfaction.

♦ In circumstances where the task/role is clear and structured, supportive leader behavior is not necessary to improve member satisfaction or performance.

♦ Supportive leadership is more appropriate in situations where the task/role is not satisfying to members; the assumption here is that such leader behavior helps, in part, to compensate for the unpleasant nature of the task/role. Directive behavior in such circumstances decreases member satisfaction, but may be necessary to motivate members to accomplish the task/role.

Hackman and Oldham (1975) analyze specific jobs in terms of the types and variety of skills demanded by the task, the clarity of the task, the significance of the task, the level of authority and feedback associated with the task, and the growth needs of persons assigned the job. It is clear that task characteristics are expected to interact with the needs and interests of the person assigned the task.

The theory of job design (Hackman & Oldham, 1975) indicates that this interaction influences the staff member's feelings about work (affective states) as well as their productivity. One of the main assumptions behind job design theory is that the task and the employee need to be reasonably matched for optimum outcomes. By implication, this suggests that it is inappropriate to delegate a highly significant, obtuse task to an inexperienced, unskilled staff member without substantial guidance, facilitation, and oversight by an accomplished staff member or administrator. Indeed, Yeaman (1994) asserts that assigning tasks only to qualified personnel is a tenet of leadership ethics.

From another perspective, Fisher (1993) and Lay (1992) categorize tasks on the basis of their intrinsic attractiveness to the employee. Perceptions of intrinsic attractiveness strengthen as perceptions increase that decisions/tasks are directly work related; there is typically less interest in policy-oriented decisions (Liverpool, 1990). Teachers report that tasks and decisions dealing directly with instructors and instructional matters are those that are most intrinsically attractive (Conway, 1984; Gips & Bredeson, 1984; Mohrman, Cooke, & Mohrman, 1978; Schneider, 1984; Smith, 1981), and that participating in instructional tasks and decisions seems to increase teacher satisfaction (Conway, 1984).

Similarly, Puffer (1989) classifies tasks based on the degree to which they are boring or difficult. The relationship between these classification schemes and those used by Simon (1947) and Bridges (1967) in the analysis of zone of acceptance are conceptually similar.

Bridges used the concepts of relevance and expertise to guide administrators in their thinking about appropriate levels of participation in decision making (see Chapter 3). Relevance refers to the level of interest and perceived impact a member attaches to a given decision or task. It is arguable that the most critical characteristic of decisions and/or tasks is the degree of relevance to prospective delegatees. Recalling earlier discussions regarding the zone of acceptance, decisions/tasks are not relevant when the member or group has little interest and perceives that there will be little personal or work-related impact. On the other hand, those decisions/tasks that might impact the member, and which are of interest to the member, are considered to be outside the zone of acceptance, or relevant.

Implicitly, Bridges' model attempts to match the nature of the task to the employee. It is feasible to argue that relevance is, in part, embodied in attractive, stimulating tasks, and that expertise is related to the conceptual difficulty of the task. These task classification schemes are not entirely new, and it is generally accepted that organization members should be involved when decisions and tasks are relevant to them (Bridges, 1967; Simon, 1947; Taylor & Card, 1985; Vroom & Yetton, 1973).

This information can be summarized in the participation-delegation model as shown in Figure 5.2.

EXPANDING THE MODEL: A GROUP EXERCISE

Divide your colleagues or classmates into two groups. Using Bill's "to do list," one group should assume that Bill plans to delegate each of the "to do" items to a first-year teacher who is

FIGURE 5.2. PARTICIPATION LEVEL FOR MEMBERS
BASED ON INTERACTION BETWEEN TASKS AND INDIVIDUALS

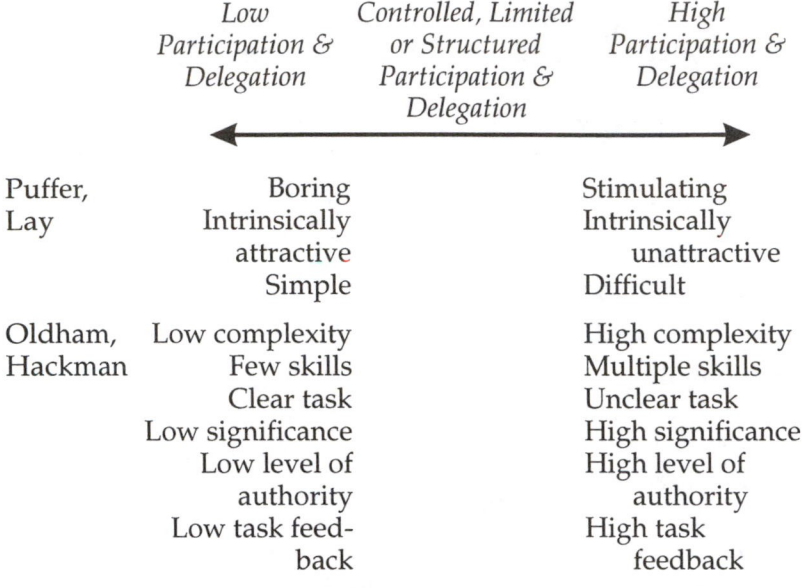

	Low Participation & Delegation	*Controlled, Limited or Structured Participation & Delegation*	*High Participation & Delegation*
Puffer, Lay	Boring Intrinsically attractive Simple		Stimulating Intrinsically unattractive Difficult
Oldham, Hackman	Low complexity Few skills Clear task Low significance Low level of authority Low task feed- back		High complexity Multiple skills Unclear task High significance High level of authority High task feedback

a recruit from industry and has come to the school as a provisionally certified teacher. The other group should assume that Bill plans to delegate each task to a 15-year teaching veteran, who is teacher of the year and who also runs summer school.

Apply the information presented in Figure 5.2 to assess the probability of success for Bill's delegation strategy. Explain your analysis and propose an improved alternative, if one is warranted, along with a rationale.

Present your analysis and conclusions to the other groups for reaction.

SUMMARY

Tasks that may be delegated differ in ways that have important bearings on plans to delegate. These differences interact with the attributes of staff members and groups to whom they may be assigned. Delegation contingencies associated with the individual are explored in greater detail in Chapter 6, while contingencies associated with groups are explored in Chapter 7.

Both the differences in tasks and the interaction of these differences with specific employee attributes should be factored into an administrator's decisions about participative decision-making and delegation.

APPLYING YOUR KNOWLEDGE

1. Work out a plan for you and a group of your colleagues or classmates to meet separately with other school administrators. Each of you should explain to the host administrator what you are learning in this chapter. Ask if you might sample the items on the administrator's "to do list." Use these items as a basis for applying all of the materials in this chapter. Compare your list with those of your colleagues or classmates to note similarities and differences in lists and analyses.

2. Discuss the material in this chapter with a teacher. Can this material be used as a basis for teacher decisions about instructional strategies such as cooperative learning groups, integrated lesson design, and so forth?

3. Develop a list of five plausible school tasks with a group of your colleagues or classmates. Draw from the chapter the most appropriate descriptors of these tasks. Make a checklist of descriptors in *either/or* terms from Figures 5.1 (p. 56) and 5.2. Rate the five tasks in terms of these descriptors and ask another administrator to share his or her ratings with you. Compare your individual and collective results with the group.

6

PARTICIPANT CONTINGENCIES AND THEIR EFFECT ON DELEGATION

SETTING THE STAGE

THE SITUATION

Jerry Wills, principal at Sandlewood High, gave the faculty and staff advance notice that everyone would be deeply involved with the upcoming reaccreditation by the Southern Association of Colleges and Schools (SACS). This morning, he posted a list of the chairs and members for 10 SACS committees in the lounge.

An administrative intern, Susan, arrives at the lounge to examine the list just in time to hear this conversation:

Sam: "I could care less about facilities and what do I know about it anyway? Wonder if I can get this changed?"

Barbara: "Maybe we could change. I teach math and handling all the knotty issues pertaining to humanities curricula is not my cup of tea."

Jill: "I wouldn't mind being a member of the humanities committee, but I really can't accept the responsibility of chairing the steering committee. I'm taking care of an aging parent and my hands are full. This assignment just won't work for me."

Henry: "You know, I love keeping a hundred balls in the air. It is some kind of weird challenge to me, sort of like scheduling, which I also like to do. Maybe I could chair the steering committee instead of serving as a member on the support services committee."

Ramona: "How in the world am I going to chair the writing committee? Who's going to handle the school newspaper, cheerleaders, and bus duty? Managing all of this at one time is just not feasible."

Celia: "Who cares about this stupid accreditation anyway? I'm out of here the first decent job opportunity I get."

Sam: "I guess we all need to talk to Jerry about this."

YOUR THOUGHTS ARE?

With your colleagues or classmates, identify a list of individual attributes that seem to be influencing faculty reactions to their delegated roles and assignments. If you were Jerry, how might you have factored this information into your planning of SACS assignments? What can and should Susan do with what she has inadvertently learned?

INTRODUCTION

Setting the Stage illustrates how important it is for administrators to consider faculty and staff attributes in delegation. Human beings are different in many ways! Such an observation seems almost trite until one considers that individual differences are important variables in decision making and delegation. Perceptions, beliefs, expertise, experiences, commitment, and information-processing skills are not all alike (Bryant & MacPhail-Wilcox, 1988).

These differences create another important class of contingencies that impact the delegation of work and decision making. Indeed, they influence not only the delegation and decision-making processes, but, more importantly, the outcomes of these very processes.

As we saw in Chapter 5, all tasks and decisions are not alike either. Each requires different capacities to accomplish it effectively. In other words, different types of tasks and decisions call for different kinds of people and the match between individual and task is often the deciding factor in successful delegation. Indeed, Barrett's research (1978) found that as disparity between an individual's preference for a task and the task's demands increase, job outcomes decline.

This chapter describes how selected staff attributes can affect administrative effectiveness in delegation. Opportunities to apply and expand your knowledge of these important contingencies occur throughout the chapter.

SELECTED INDIVIDUAL ATTRIBUTE CONTINGENCIES AND DELEGATION

What are some of the important differences among individuals to be factored into delegation and participative decision making plans? Literature reporting on direct analysis of the effects of personal attributes on delegation and participative decision making for particular types of tasks is limited. It is an area rich with opportunities for new research which can improve administrative practice.

For simplicity, a case can be made that there are three groups of individual attribute contingencies relevant to our topic. These attribute contingencies are classified here on the basis of differences in information processing, expertise, and motivation or commitment to task accomplishment.

INFORMATION-PROCESSING CONTINGENCIES

Individuals vary in both their preferences for, understanding of, and responses to complex decision and task circumstances (Avolio, Alexander, Barrett, & Sterns, 1979; Schroder, Driver, & Streufert, 1967). Decision making, problem solving, critical analysis and evaluation, scheduling, and the like are information intensive tasks that require different information processing capabilities. Studies of effective decision makers (Bridges, 1967) demonstrate that they tend to put substantial emphasis and time on understanding the problem before seeking a solution. Less-effective decision makers do just the opposite.

In a comprehensive review, Bryant and MacPhail-Wilcox (1988) report that numerous individual perceptual, cognitive process, and dispositional differences influence both decision-making processes and decision outcomes. Variables accounting for differences in perception include field dependence/independence, Myers-Briggs information-processing preferences, and reflective/impulsive orientations. Attributes influencing information-processing behaviors include conceptual complexity, heuristic/analytic approaches to data, concrete/abstract or active/reflective styles, and preferences for single/multiple sources of data and feasible solutions or decisions. They argue that because these style attributes are not distributed equally in the population, it is critical for administrators to match individuals with tasks or to be widely inclusive in establishing work groups. Figure 6.1 (pp. 68–69) outlines the essential relationships between individual information processing variables and decision outcomes.

One of these individual attributes, conceptual complexity, we describe briefly to illustrate how it relates to an individual's information processing ability. Conceptual systems theory and research (Avolio et al, 1979) illustrates that people differ in conceptual complexity. These differences affect their communication, problem solving, and decision-making behaviors in predictable ways.

Conceptual complexity is a macroinformation-processing characteristic. It is reflected in an individual's capacity to handle a high rate and load of information, to discriminate between and among pieces of information, and to integrate seemingly disparate pieces of information—all of which might be considered metainformation-processing components.

This kind of research would suggest that tasks and decisions which are replete with conflicting information, those requiring the capacity to discriminate carefully among pieces of information, and those which will occur with much input from many people will be more effectively handled by persons of high conceptual complexity. Furthermore, it is possible to get an approximation of a staff member's conceptual complexity by observing his or her communication, problem solving, and decision-making behaviors.

The existence of attribute contingencies suggests that the person to whom a task or decision is delegated will be a key determinant of how effectively and efficiently it will be handled. In the absence of certain knowledge about the effects of these attributes on performance, inclusiveness is a viable alternative for insuring that needed information processing skills are available for complex tasks and decisions.

INFORMATION PROCESSING CONTINGENCIES: APPLYING YOUR KNOWLEDGE

1. Select one of the individual attributes described in this section for library review. Present a summary review to colleagues or classmates and a set of reasoned hypotheses about how the attribute might influence success on a routine and then on a novel task drawn from the previous chapter.

2. With a group of colleagues or classmates, discuss if and how this knowledge illuminates the lounge discussion presented in Setting the Stage. What difference might it have made in Jerry's delegated assignments?

EXPERTISE CONTINGENCIES

The successful accomplishment of tasks requires both specific information-processing skills and contextual expertise. For our purposes, context is the environment, surrounding conditions, or matrix in which something occurs. So, contextual expertise, as used here, reflects the expertise and experience an individual has with respect to a particular subject, problem, or task that they may be assigned.

As we noted earlier, Bridges (1967) and others (e.g., Hackman & Oldham, 1975; Hersey & Blanchard, 1982) contend that the level of skill, the depth of experience, and the expertise associated with particular tasks are important individual attribute contingencies. In the previous discussion of Hersey and Blanchard's follower-based theory (1982), it was observed that "task

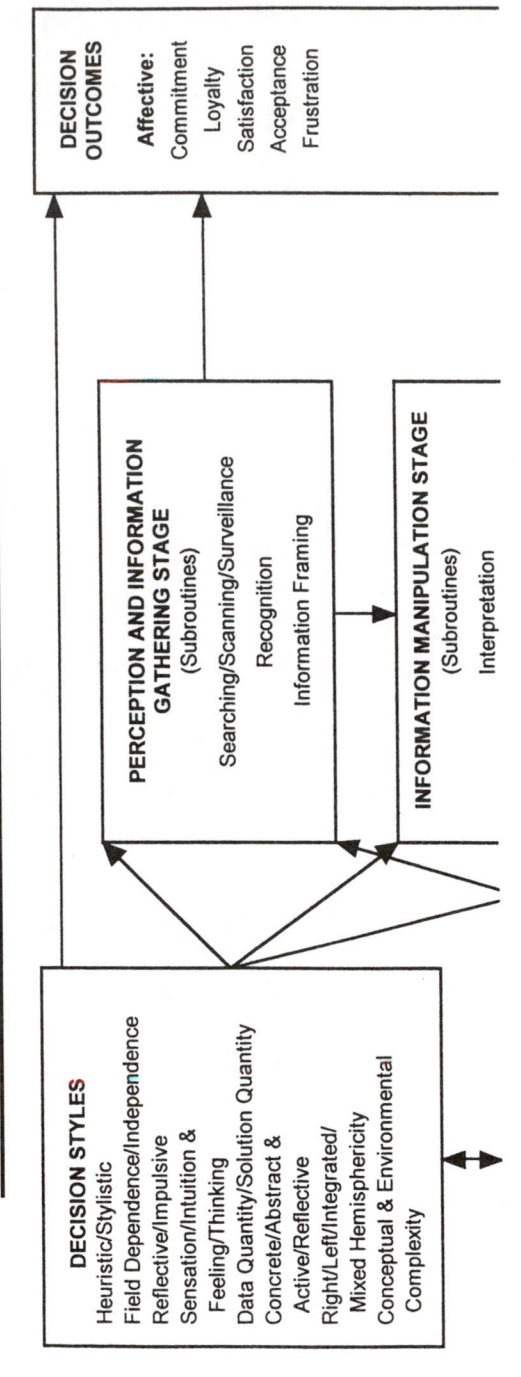

FIGURE 6.1. THE IMPACT OF INDIVIDUAL PERCEPTUAL, COGNITIVE PROCESS, AND DISPOSITIONAL DIFFERENCES UPON DECISION-MAKING PROCESSES AND OUTCOMES (BRYANT & MACPHAIL-WILCOX, 1988)

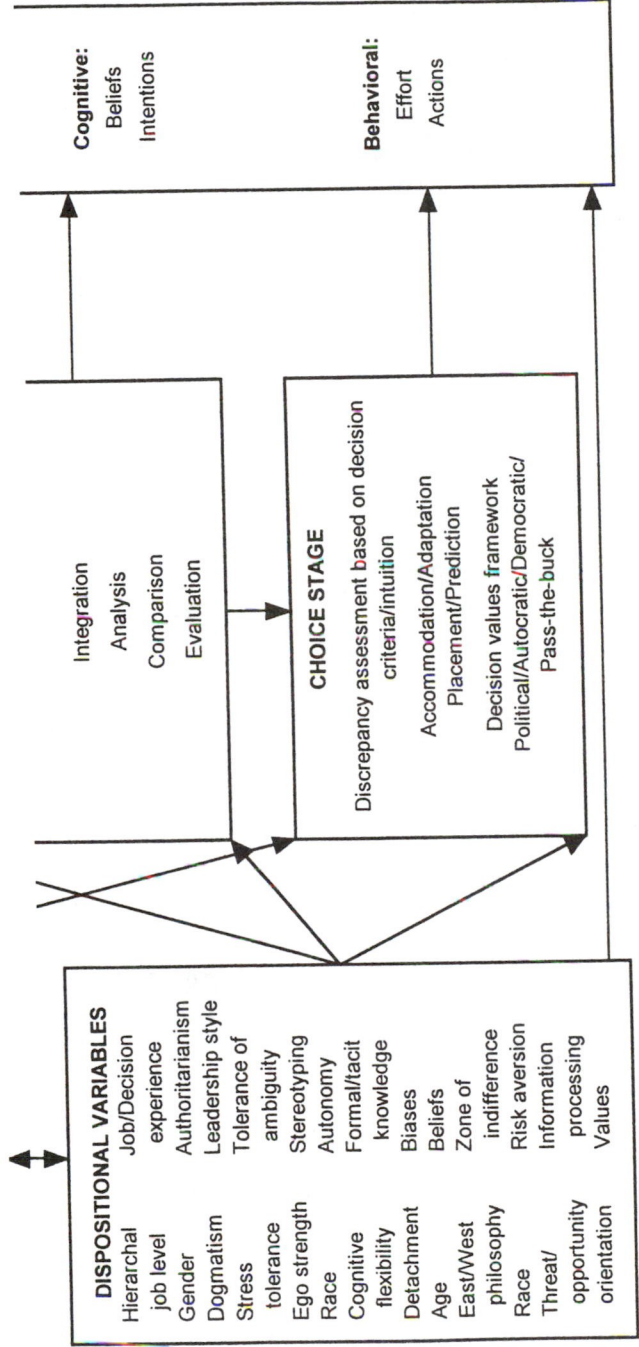

maturity" will not only vary from individual to individual, but also from task to task with the same individual. More recently, studies have demonstrated that novice and expert problem solvers (Berliner, 1986; Puffer, 1989) vary in the efficiency and effectiveness with which they solve problems, both of which are concerns for an effective delegator.

The challenge for the leader is to become effective at analyzing the expertise of potential participants in a decision making or delegation process. Such analysis has implications for the leader's subsequent decisions regarding assignment of tasks and decisions. In the following Applying Your Knowledge, consider the manner in which participant expertise influences decisions about their participation.

EXPERTISE CONTINGENCIES: APPLYING YOUR KNOWLEDGE

1. Return to Setting the Stage and identify instances in which the speaker's comments suggest that expertise contingencies may underlie the degree of willingness to accept the committee assignment.

2. What sources of information might a leader draw upon to determine the level of expertise for a prospective participant to whom a task or decision might be assigned?

3. If a principal was considering an initiative that would create a schoolwide integrated reading curriculum, to what degree would the principal be justified in excluding any staff member from initial discussions based on differences in individual attributes? Defend your answer.

4. Maria is a high school principal and is preparing to hire a new assistant principal. She wants to include some parents and staff members in the interview and recommendation process. However, she is alarmed by another principal's account of a similar situation in which parent participants in the interview process asked a female applicant whether or not her family responsibilities might interfere with

her need to supervise night-time activities at school. Another applicant was extended an invitation to join a particular local church, should he or she be selected. Maria is now seriously questioning the value of inviting parent representatives to participate in the interviews. What might she do to avoid the problems experienced by the other principal and still adhere to her original plan?

MOTIVATION CONTINGENCIES

Few contingencies impact the effective completion of a task by an individual, or an individual's effective participation in decision making, more than that individual's motivation and commitment. Thus, effective delegation requires more than matching the task demands with the individual cognitive abilities and expertise of staff. People vary in their motivation and commitment (Duke, 1994) to participate in particular activities and assignments; tasks are differentially motivating and interesting. Effective delegators recognize that it is important for staff to be enthusiastic, interested, and satisfied with their assignments.

A very important motivational consideration is the degree to which decisions and delegated tasks are seen as *relevant* by the individuals to whom they might be assigned (Barnard, 1938; Bridges, 1967; Simon, 1947.) The enthusiasm with which a delegated task or decision-making opportunity is undertaken depends, in part, on how relevant or interesting the task is to a particular staff member. While other decisions and tasks may matter to prospective delegatees, those with direct work-related impact appear to be most relevant (Liverpool, 1990). Thus, a leader may vary his or her decision regarding the assignment of a task or decision depending upon the degree to which a participant appears to be interested or committed. There are also times when an administrator must arouse interest and motivation before staff are willing to engage in a specific task (Avolio et al., 1979).

Hackman and Oldham (1975) propose that job characteristics impact individual motivation. These authors assert that core job characteristics such as the level and variety of skills required, the clarity of the task(s), task significance, autonomy, and task feedback impact critical psychological states. These psychological states include perceptions of the meaningfulness of work, sense of responsibility for work outcomes, and awareness of the actual work results. The critical psychological states in turn influence important individual attributes such as work motivation, job satisfaction, and job effectiveness (Figure 6.2).

Individuals differ in the degree to which achievement, affiliation, and power motivate them (McClelland, 1985), sometimes in unanticipated ways. For instance, Puffer (1989) found that persons with a high need for achievement, successful prior performance on a similar task, and heavy workloads were more likely to complete work on time and effectively than those with opposing circumstances. This seems to validate the old adage that "if you want something done, delegate it to a busy person or the one you always call on." Yet, others (Avolio et al, 1979; Fisher, 1993) report that performance on a repetitive task decreases over time, irrespective of age. Similarly, Katz (1978) and Gardner (1986) contend that the initial stages of learning and responsive implementation accompanying motivated behavior are followed by an unresponsive stage characterized by boredom and the absence of activation.

Such seemingly contradictory findings suggest that prior success and experience with a specific task (contextual expertise contingencies) are insufficient bases for making delegation decisions! Research by McClelland (1985) suggests that persons motivated by achievement like to define and solve problems, whereas those motivated by affiliation like to confirm their own beliefs and work in a relatively certain or stable environment where they can insure the quality of personal relations. Staff motivated by power, on the other hand, like to exercise control, influence, and authority. So, in addition to task expertise, effective delegators need to include an analysis of individual motivation into task and decision assignments.

Equity in delegation also affects motivation. Individuals hold perceptions of their own skills, effort, and productivity relative to those of other persons with similar status. Based upon these perceptions and perceptions of task demands, an individual will also possess certain beliefs about the rewards to which he or she is entitled, and the rewards to which others are entitled. Perceived discrepancies between these rewards can affect

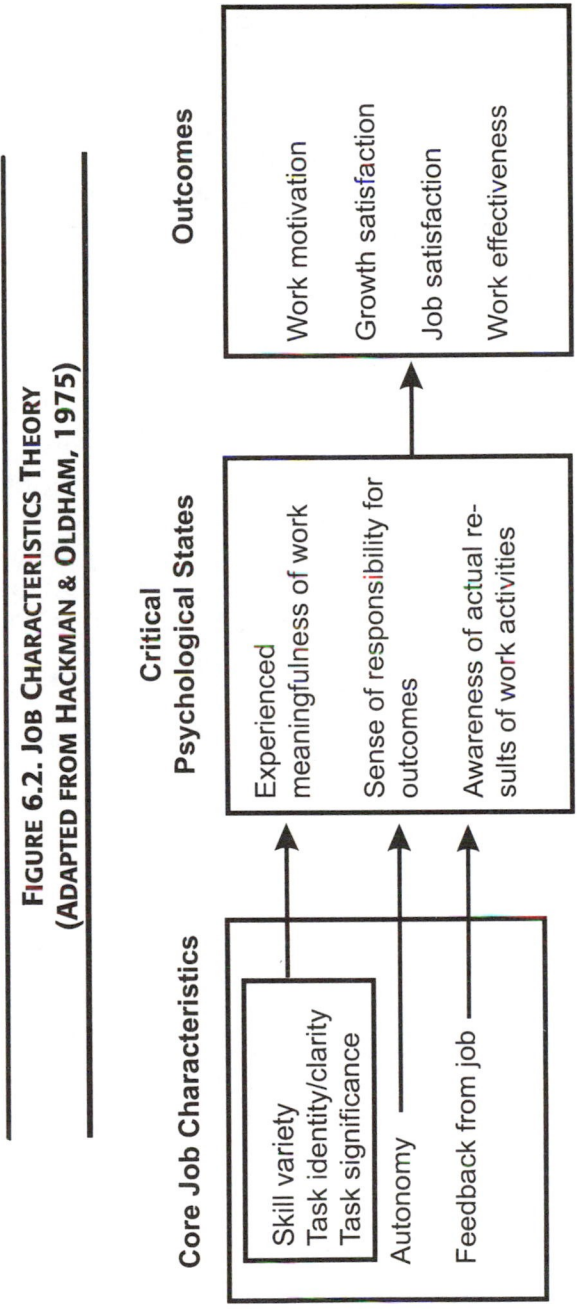

FIGURE 6.2. JOB CHARACTERISTICS THEORY (ADAPTED FROM HACKMAN & OLDHAM, 1975)

Core Job Characteristics

- Skill variety
- Task identity/clarity
- Task significance
- Autonomy
- Feedback from job

Critical Psychological States

- Experienced meaningfulness of work
- Sense of responsibility for outcomes
- Awareness of actual results of work activities

Outcomes

- Work motivation
- Growth satisfaction
- Job satisfaction
- Work effectiveness

the member's motivation, satisfaction, and perceptions of equity in the organization (Adams, 1963; Tyler, 1991).

It should be evident by now that motivation and commitment are influenced in many ways. Work activities that support personal growth, relate to an individual's central life interests, and transcend personal welfare issues promote commitment (Duke, 1994). Conversely, burnout theory tells us that physical, emotional, and mental exhaustion are in part a reaction to circumstances in which these conditions are not met—conditions over which the administrator has some control (Moracco, D'Arienzo, & Danforth, 1983).

There are no guaranteed formulas for increasing motivation, but research does provide some helpful hints. For example, ensuring some sense of control over work assignments and decisions, such as could be derived from advance discussion about potential assignments, optional assignments, and the willingness/ability to take on assignments, has been shown to strengthen commitment and a sense of efficacy (Ashton, 1985). Similarly, combining goal setting and feedback on work activities has been shown to enhance performance on assignments (Watson, 1983).

Whether organization members will act in the interest of organizational goals is yet another contingency affecting delegation decisions. Individuals have personal needs and goals that they seek to fulfill in the work setting. In instances when these personal goals run contrary to organizational goals, there is a question as to whether the member can be trusted to place the organization's aims above the member's own. The degree to which the leader perceives that individuals can be trusted to act in the organization's interests can and should be factored into a leader's choices regarding the involvement of members in decision making and decision implementation (Taylor & Card, 1985; Vroom & Yetton, 1973).

MOTIVATION CONTINGENCIES:
APPLYING YOUR KNOWLEDGE

1. Megan Tindle is a social studies teacher at Las Piedras Middle School. She holds a masters in school administration, and for several years has sought extra

administrative duties. The principal has been happy to delegate certain assignments; for example, Megan supervises the school's transportation program. She arrives early to monitor the area where the buses arrive. During her planning period, she handles bus discipline, transportation-related paperwork, and related phone calls. These duties are draining and require significant extra time, but Megan is hopeful that these efforts will increase her prospects for becoming an assistant principal. During the years, however, she has been passed over several times, and has noticed that a lot of the administrative promotions have gone to candidates from outside the school district. She has decided to not accept the transportation duties next year, and to devote more time to her teaching assignments and to interests away from school. Which theory(ies) of motivation might explain Megan's loss of interest in performing the transportation duties? Discuss your conclusions with others, either classmates or colleagues.

2. Reading scores have been less than satisfactory at Leesburg Elementary School, and the staff is studying a number of reforms to improve achievement. One idea that is heavily favored by the principal and the parent advisory council is to extend the school day by 30 minutes and to use the extra time to provide additional learning opportunities in reading. Upon learning of this particular proposal, Ms. Hinnant, a veteran teacher of 12 years, volunteered to chair the committee that will investigate its merits. The principal knows Ms. Hinnant is very competent, and readily delegates this responsibility to her. Over the next several days, Ms. Hinnant pulls together several articles and pieces of research, each of which suggests that more time is not necessarily an effective strategy for improving reading. Articles which draw a contrary conclusion are ignored; Ms. Hinnant even removes some from

the professional library shelf. On the night before the committee's first meeting, several parents, at Ms. Hinnant's encouragement, call other committee members to say how displeased they are by the potential disruption of their family schedules that would result from an extension of the school day. Not surprisingly, the committee moves rapidly to a recommendation not to pursue an extension of the school day.

With others, consider the theories of motivation that help in the analysis of this scenario. What strategies might aid school leaders in preventing such situations?

3. Return to the Setting the Stage vignette at the beginning of this chapter. One of Jerry's assistant principals, Abram Lawson, has asked to be assigned as an ex officio member of the steering committee and of several other key committees. Jerry is pleased to have such representation on the committees, because his schedule prevents him from attending all but a few meetings. However, as time goes on, he learns that Abram has been outspoken in meetings of the committees, often dominating the conversation, and pushing his own recommendations.

Analyze the assistant principal's leadership style. Which theories of motivation help in the analysis of this situation?

4. Resume your consideration of the Setting the Stage vignette at the beginning of this chapter. How might what you've learned in this chapter influence your decisions about delegating committee assignments if you were in Jerry's position?

DELEGATING TO INDIVIDUALS: A SYNTHESIS MODEL OF A LEADER'S RESPONSE TO INFORMATION PROCESSING, EXPERTISE, AND MOTIVATION CONTINGENCIES

Figure 6.3 highlights the decision-making junctures that are confronted by an administrator as the administrator makes determinations about the individuals who will be assigned certain tasks and asked to participate in certain decisions. While this is only one formula for tying together a complex set of leadership variables, it does summarize the major individual attribute contingencies associated with delegation and decision making. It also suggests courses of action depending on the leader's assessment of individuals with regard to key delegation considerations. The model also examines the potential consequences of certain leader decisions.

SUMMARY

Individual differences associated with decision making and delegation include:

- ♦ Information-processing contingencies, including the conceptual complexity of the individual;
- ♦ Expertise contingencies such as those related to the task maturity of the individual;
- ♦ Motivational contingencies, including:
  - The degree to which the individual perceives decisions or tasks to be relevant;
  - The affinity and or commitment of the individual for given tasks;
- ♦ Degree to which task decisions or tasks are congruent with individual's interests and needs for achievement;
- ♦ Degree to which the individual feels that there is equity in the distribution of responsibility for decision making and tasks; and

FIGURE 6.3. A SCHOOL LEADER'S GUIDE: INDIVIDUAL CONTINGENCIES

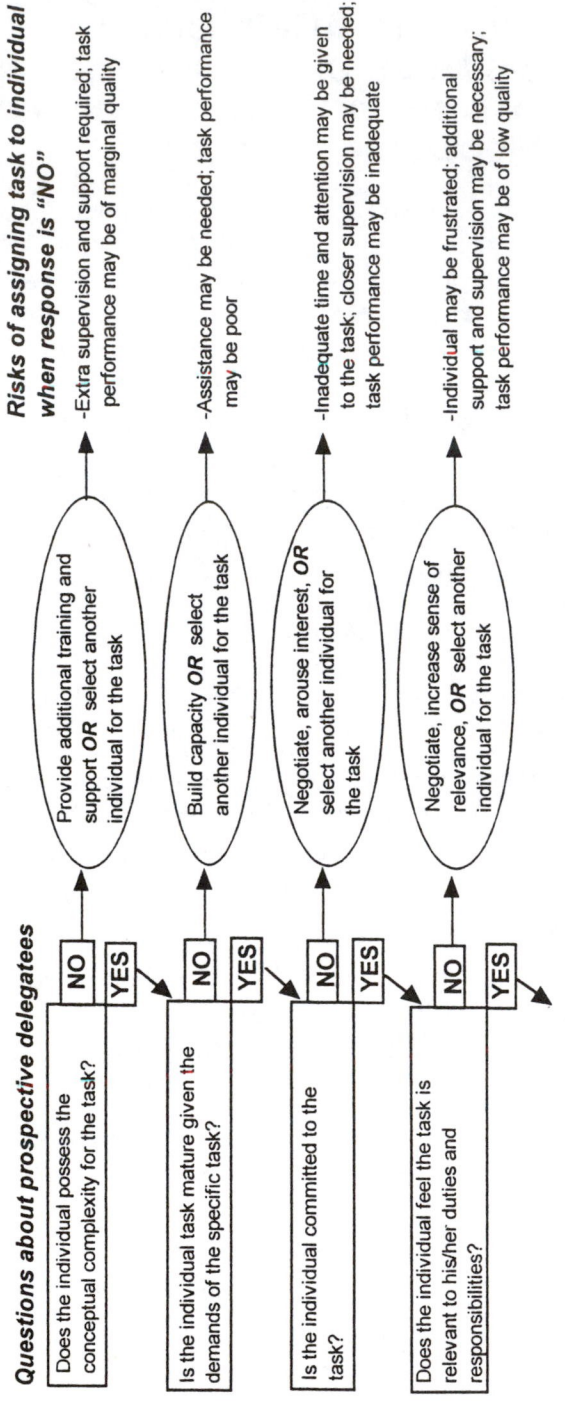

Questions about prospective delegatees

Risks of assigning task to individual when response is "NO"

Does the individual possess the conceptual complexity for the task?

NO → Provide additional training and support OR select another individual for the task → -Extra supervision and support required; task performance may be of marginal quality

YES

Is the individual task mature given the demands of the specific task?

NO → Build capacity OR select another individual for the task → -Assistance may be needed; task performance may be poor

YES

Is the individual committed to the task?

NO → Negotiate, arouse interest, OR select another individual for the task → -Inadequate time and attention may be given to the task; closer supervision may be needed; task performance may be inadequate

YES

Does the individual feel the task is relevant to his/her duties and responsibilities?

NO → Negotiate, increase sense of relevance, OR select another individual for the task → -Individual may be frustrated; additional support and supervision may be necessary; task performance may be of low quality

YES

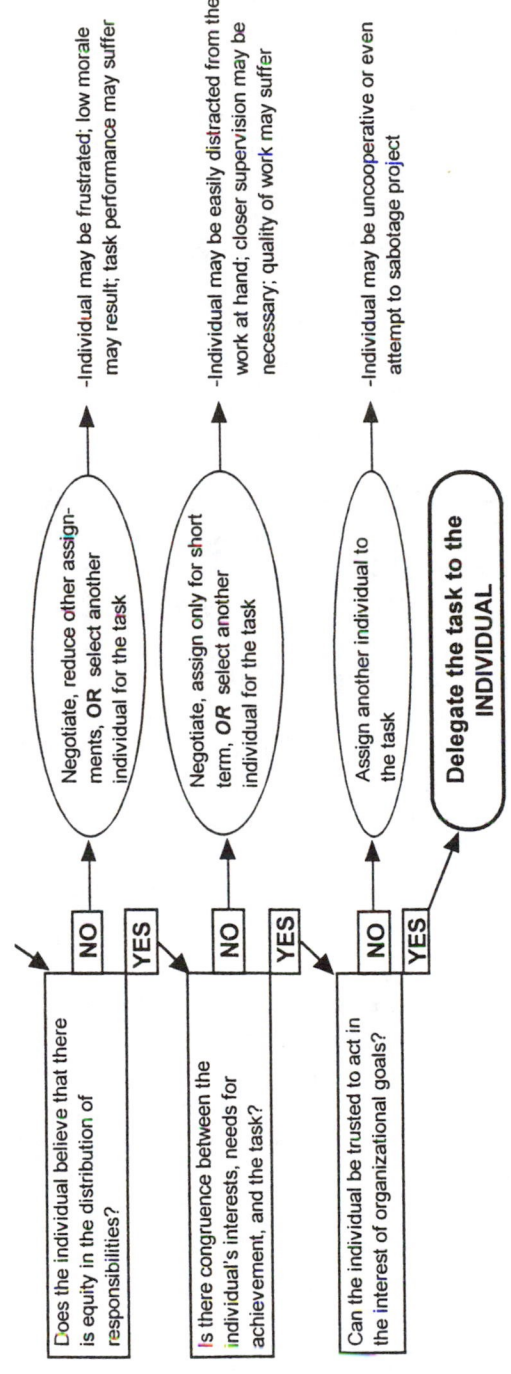

Does the individual believe that there is equity in the distribution of responsibilities?

NO → Negotiate, reduce other assignments, **OR** select another individual for the task → -Individual may be frustrated; low morale may result; task performance may suffer

YES

Is there congruence between the individual's interests, needs for achievement, and the task?

NO → Negotiate, assign only for short term, *OR* select another individual for the task → -Individual may be easily distracted from the work at hand; closer supervision may be necessary; quality of work may suffer

YES

Can the individual be trusted to act in the interest of organizational goals?

NO → Assign another individual to the task → -Individual may be uncooperative or even attempt to sabotage project

YES → Delegate the task to the INDIVIDUAL

♦ Congruence between the individual's goals and the aims of the organization.

A thoughtful school leader will use knowledge of such contingencies, and insights regarding the individuals with whom the leader works, as decisions are made regarding the delegation of decisions and tasks.

EXTENDING YOUR KNOWLEDGE

1. Obtain instrumentation that will assess some of the attributes identified in Figure 6.1 (p. 68) (Bryant & MacPhail-Wilcox model). Conduct a self-assessment to gain some insight into your own information processing preferences.

2. With colleagues or classmates, come up with several "real world" examples of circumstances in which school leaders make decisions about delegating tasks and including others in decision making. Analyze these circumstances by applying the model outlined in Figure 6.3 (pp. 78–79). How helpful is the model? Are there additional questions or steps needed in the model to address the circumstances in some of the examples you've developed? Are some questions or steps unnecessary? Are some questions or steps more difficult to analyze than others? How would you go about acquiring the information needed to analyze each question and step?

3. Invest some time researching management models that appear to be consistent with some of the suggestions for strengthening information processing, expertise, and motivation among staff members. Among the models that you investigate, consider the total quality management theories of W. Edwards Deming, the follower-based leadership model of Hersey and Blanchard (1982), and the theories of motivation such as House and Mitchell's (1974) path-goal theory.

7

GROUP CONTINGENCIES AND THEIR EFFECT ON DELEGATION

SETTING THE STAGE

THE SITUATION

Andy Bennett, principal at West Stratford Elementary School, has become convinced of the benefits of a nongraded, continuous progress model for promotion in what would traditionally be a K–3 school. In such a model, students are not assigned to grade levels, but are simply designated as first-, second-, third-, or fourth-year students. Students progress through the program of studies over the four years at the pace that works best for each student. Multiage grouping places students at similar stages of progress in the same classroom. A student experiencing difficulty is not retained at the end of the year; instead, the student may attend a summer program for extra assistance, and, at the beginning of the new school year, may resume studies at the point where the student left off. The only point at which retention is an issue is when decisions must be made concerning whether to hold fourth-year students experiencing difficulty over for a fifth year at West Stratford.

Andy and the faculty have engaged in sufficient research on the nongraded system, and in sufficient dialogue with the community so that they are, with a few exceptions, ready to initiate the model at West Stratford. There is a great deal of work to be done: the curriculum must be organized for the continuous progress format, a related assessment program must be developed, a parent orientation and ongoing communication process must be organized, a system for reporting student progress must be developed, staff training activities must be scheduled— the list of decisions and tasks is almost endless! Andy and the faculty/parent leadership council decide to divide into teams to make recommendations and to carry out the various tasks associated with the new program.

Andy realizes the magnitude of the work before him and the faculty. He is also keenly aware that, while the majority of staff members support the innovation, there are skeptics in the ranks. Some have done enough research and heard enough community criticism that they are genuinely concerned that the new model may not be in the best interest of the school.

YOUR THOUGHTS ARE?

Andy faces a daunting task in organizing teams for the various decisions and tasks that are necessary for successful implementation of the new continuous progress model. What factors should he consider in assigning individuals to the various teams? What training in group processes should be provided to team members? How should teams report their progress, be monitored, and be supervised? With others, consider the responses to these questions and to other issues that will confront Andy in organizing teams to carry out the necessary work.

INTRODUCTION

Chapter 6 examined the relationship of individual differences to effective delegation. Frequently, individuals act as members of formal and informal groups in work settings. Just as individuals vary, one group may differ from another in terms of collective expertise, experience, motivation, and other variables. Group participation creates additional contingencies because the behavior of individuals in groups is often different than in isolation. Just as there are distinctions among individuals, there are differences in group attributes which have an effect upon decision making and delegation. Such differences have implications for a leader's decisions regarding delegation and the participation of groups in decision making.

School leaders frequently assign responsibility for decision making and tasks to groups rather than to individuals. There are a number of advantages to such assignments, including:

♦ The opportunity to focus the expertise and experience of multiple persons on the problem or task;

♦ The ability to spread large work assignments among several persons; and

♦ The opportunity to build the leadership and expertise of individuals who participate in and are mentored by the group.

There are also disadvantages to delegating decisions/tasks to groups. Groups possess greater potential for conflict over roles and turf. There is also the potential that groups may actually perform less capably than individuals, and groups often take more time than individuals to make decisions.

This chapter explores the practical application of research related to group characteristics in decision making and delegation. The following sections offer suggestions and guides to school leaders as they consider the impact of group differences on effective participation.

SELECTED GROUP CONTINGENCIES AND DELEGATION

School administrators often desire to delegate tasks or decisions to groups such as grade-level or departmental teams, advisory groups, standing and ad hoc committees, and so on. The most prevalent form of group empowerment is the teacher advisory group, which varies in level of formality and decision-making authority (Webster, 1994). Leader rationales for group involvement differ, but here we assume that a significant part of the motivation revolves around a sincere belief in the principles of empowerment. Delegation to groups requires an appreciation of, and the capacity to analyze the characteristics of work groups and the manner in which member interaction affects both processes and outcomes.

Just as human beings differ from one another, individual behavior can differ according to whether one is in a group or alone.

The complexities of group dynamics add an additional dimension to the administrator's analysis of to whom and under what circumstances decisions and tasks will be delegated. The quantity and quality of work and interaction within a group is affected by the nature of the group's membership and the group's collective propensities. The following sections highlight selected group contingency categories: nature of the decision/task, task maturity, cross-functionality, creativity, cohesiveness, "groupthink," and group size.

NATURE OF THE DECISION OR TASK

There are advantages to assigning some types of tasks and decisions to groups instead of individuals. For example, tasks and decisions that are novel and/or complex are frequently handled more capably by a group or team. Tasks that may consume significant time and energy may be more effectively accomplished if there are multiple persons to share the work and the responsibility.

Stoner (1961) asserts that tasks with significant risk or potential for controversy are often more appropriately assigned to a group. Similarly, groups are more likely than individuals to accept higher risks. While this is a strength of delegation to groups, it is also a potential weakness. A later section describes the problems associated with *groupthink*. One such problem is the illusion of invulnerability: members of the group are less cognizant of risks and may inflate their prospects for successful performance. A wise school leader recognizes such potential pitfalls and provides appropriate cautions to the group in high-risk circumstances.

TASK MATURITY

Just as individuals vary in their level of task maturity, groups also vary in their collective level of experience, expertise, and commitment (Carew, Parisi-Carew, & Blanchard, 1986). The productivity of groups evolves through a series of stages (Lacoursiere, 1980; Tuckman, 1965; Tuckman & Jensen 1977):

- ◆ Orientation: the stage at which the group is assigned and introduced to its tasks.

- Dissatisfaction: the stage in which actual experiences and initial expectations for the group's interaction and task responsibilities are contrasted. The duration of this stage can be minimized by early clarity regarding member roles, tasks, and expectations.

- Resolution: the stage in which major dissatisfaction is resolved, processes for accomplishing the work are developed, and norms for group interaction either evolve or are agreed upon.

- Production: the stage at which the group begins to optimize both the quality of decisions and the level of productivity.

- Termination: Lacoursiere (1980) notes that this stage applies only to temporary ad hoc committees, task forces, and the like. This stage is not pertinent to groups with ongoing responsibilities.

Various authors have referred to the first four stages of this developmental process as forming, storming, norming, and performing. No matter the terminology, it is evident that groups mature in their capacity and propensity to deliver products in response to assigned tasks. The prudent leader is sensitive to this development and works to maximize group progress toward the more productive stages.

It is important for groups to strike an appropriate balance between task focus and the focus on relationships within the group. Groups that are inordinately task-focused tend to alienate members, whereas groups that concentrate too heavily on social-emotional issues tend to accomplish less (Shaw, 1990).

Effective school leaders often view delegation and decision making in groups as an opportunity to strengthen the capacity of individuals. Assigning inexperienced and/or less competent persons to groups that include individuals possessing greater task maturity accomplishes several things. The less mature individuals have an opportunity to build expertise and experience. Performance weaknesses among less proficient members can be compensated for by the skills of more capable members. The quality of work group products is enhanced and the capacity of less proficient members is increased for future assignments.

CROSS-FUNCTIONAL EXPERTISE

Management theorists have increasingly advocated the use of teams made up of individuals representing different expertise and different subunits or departments in the organization. W. Edwards Deming, the theorist most closely associated with the quality movement in America, identifies breaking down barriers between staff areas as one of the fundamental principles by which high-performing organizations operate (Deming, 1986). Such a principle assumes that teams or groups possessing variable expertise and representing various sections within the organization will make better decisions and implement them more effectively because of the increased knowledge of the impact that decisions have across the organization. In short, it's the classic adage about "the right hand knowing what the left is doing" applied to delegation and decision making.

Schools offer tremendous potential for poor coordination across areas. Classroom teachers may be ill-advised of the goals, priorities, and activities of the guidance department; the high school social studies department may have little interaction with the science department; middle school staffs may be unfamiliar with elementary curriculum and learning objectives; transportation personnel may be out of touch with the school food services program; and so on. Cross-functional teams employed in the planning and decision-making processes help insure that knowledge is pooled and that the impact on others of decisions for one area of the school program is weighed (Monk, 1993). Such teams are more likely to avoid the pitfalls associated with *groupthink,* a concept that is detailed later.

While the potential benefits of cross-functional teaming are substantial, there are potential problems as well. Delegating decisions and tasks to representatives from various departments in the school will often be more time-consuming because meetings must be coordinated across more diverse schedules. It may also be necessary to take time to build understanding and expertise about the task/decision among those less familiar with the departments most affected. The cohesiveness of group members is likely to be weaker than would be the case among persons whose roles bring them together with greater frequency.

An effective leader considers such potential pitfalls as the leader considers delegating decisions and tasks. In spite of such problems, there is much to commend the use of groups composed of individuals who represent various sections and interests in the school organization. Such benefits as breaking down organizational barriers, coordinating efforts, employing a variety of perspectives, and lessening the potential of negative impact in one area due to the actions of another area, all argue for employing cross-functional teams in some circumstances.

CREATIVITY

Creativity is affected by the degree to which interactions in work teams are collaborative; work groups with a high level of member involvement are generally more creative (Plunkett, 1990). Bredeson (1989, p. 11) notes that staffs in empowered schools were more "positive, energetic people who ignored cynics and critics or who were able to deal with them through group consensus building." This does not mean, however, that collaborative work settings are free of conflict; Bredeson also found that, in some instances, conflict and complaining increased in empowered schools as staff members found freedom to express concerns that might previously have been stifled.

COHESIVENESS

Research studies suggest a relationship between the cohesiveness of group members and the quality of their performance. However, researchers vary in their findings regarding the optimal level of cohesiveness. Some have concluded that highly cohesive groups make better decisions and perform at a higher level (Evans & Dion, 1991; Mullen, Anthony, Salas, & Driskell, 1994; Mullen & Copper, 1994). Others have concluded that optimal decision making and productivity occur when group cohesiveness is at a moderate level (Callaway & Esser, 1984).

Bredeson (1989) noted the positive energy of staff in empowered schools; he also observed that such staff members tended to discount the opinions of critics. While the ability to move ahead in the face of cynics is commendable, some precautions are warranted. Janis (1982) describes a phenomenon, which he labels "groupthink," in which group cohesiveness actually impairs decision quality and group performance.

GROUPTHINK

It is generally accepted that there are benefits to assigning some types of tasks to groups, committees, or teams. However, as groups move from the initial stages of their development, and mature in the quality of their relationships and productivity, a potential danger arises from the very cohesiveness that has developed. Janis (1982) describes this propensity as groupthink, a level of conformity in thinking among group members that actually imperils the quality of the group's decision making and performance. Hoy and Miskel (1991) summarize the elements of groupthink as follows:

- The illusion of invulnerability: members of the group are less cognizant of risks, and may inflate their prospects for successful performance.
- Collective rationalization: logic that is inconsistent with that of the group is ignored or discredited.
- The illusion of morality: the group assumes that agreement among the members is an assurance of the "rightness" of the decisions and actions taken; ethical problems may not be apparent.
- Excessive stereotyping: persons or groups who are not members of the group in question may be typified in negative ways.
- The pressure for conformity: to avoid appearing disloyal, members may resist raising concerns about the group's positions, aims, or commitments.
- Self-censorship: the cohesiveness of the group exerts a pressure on individuals to refrain from divergent thinking, verbalizing, and acting.
- The illusion of unanimity: because the pressure for conformity and the tendency towards self-censorship inhibit positions that run counter to that of the

group, dissent is rare, and the silence of potential dissenters is viewed as asset.

♦ Mind guards: some individuals in the group are in a position to withhold information from the rest and act to insulate their colleagues from input that might threaten the group's existing positions, aims, or commitments.

A number of variables affect the propensity of a group to engage in groupthink. Group cohesiveness, while certainly desirable and necessary to productivity, exerts pressure for conformity. The presence in the group of charismatic leaders, whose opinions are significantly influential, can further stifle dissent (Hoy & Miskel, 1991). The pressures and stress associated with severe criticism from external sources, such as parents, community organizations, or political leaders, may generate a "circle the wagons" mentality.

The possibility of groupthink needn't prompt a thoughtful school leader to forego the positive potential of groups for decision making and task completion. Janis (1985), Miranda (1994), and others have proposed a number of antidotes to groupthink. Figure 7.1 summarizes the most prominent recommendations for leaders who wish to maximize group productivity while preserving an appropriate level of cohesiveness.

GROUP SIZE

Group size is an additional consideration in delegation. Mullen and Copper's analysis of multiple studies suggests that cohesive small groups are generally more productive than larger groups (1994). Shaw (1990) suggests that group size should vary according to purpose; small groups of 5–9 members are more effective for decision making, while larger groups of 10–30 members are better suited to brainstorming or generating new ideas. Wheelan and McKeage (1993) caution, however, that large groups are more likely to experience conflict, and less likely to generate participation, cohesion, and actual work products. Sato (1988) adds the element of trust as a criterion in determining group size; members of smaller groups are more likely

FIGURE 7.1. *THINK* AHEAD TO AVOID GROUPTHINK (ADAPTED FROM JANIS (1985) & MIRANDA (1994))

Groupthink poses threats to the quality of a group's decision making and task implementation. The following recommendations can help school leaders and group participants avoid such problems. The methods are referred to as the THINK strategy, a deliberate play against the word groupthink.

T eaching group participants about the nature and risks inherent in groupthink can help them avoid such pitfalls.

H eterogeneous perspectives help the group avoid unhealthy levels of conformity. It is often useful to formally assign someone the role of devil's advocate when weighing alternative decisions and courses of action.

I nformation that is drawn from external sources and that helps to reveal potential flaws in the group's proposed solutions, should be available to the group. Outside experts and stakeholder opinions are useful sources of such information.

N eutral leaders work best in most circumstances. Directive leadership can stifle creative ideas and solutions and discourage participants from countering potentially flawed decisions and actions. Leadership behaviors that counter groupthink include initially withholding personal opinions and encouraging nonconforming thought and debate among members.

K eep the decision or task at the center of the group's activities. While a healthy working atmosphere is vital and the quality of relationships is important, critical tasks and decisions have great impact on the organization and should be the primary focus of the group.

to trust and, in turn, cooperate with one another. Roberts and Bradley (1991) found that large diverse groups working on novel or complex tasks are less likely to be innovative in their solutions. Given such findings, it seems clear that group size is a significant contingency in delegation. Of course, the size of a group may not be amenable to manipulation in many instances; for example, the size of the math department of a high school is more likely to be defined by the number of math teachers than by a research-based prescription for ideal group size.

Group contingencies are obviously an important consideration for the school leader who aspires to effectiveness in delegation. To repeat, the group contingencies are:

- Nature of the decision/task
- Task maturity of the group
- Cross-functional roles and expertise of group members
- Creativity of group members
- Cohesiveness of the group
- Tendency of the group toward groupthink dysfunctions
- Size of the group

These variables pose both opportunities and challenges for the school leader who wishes to appropriately empower groups to whom decisions and tasks may be delegated. The following sections propose strategies for maximizing the effectiveness and productivity of such groups.

SUGGESTED STRATEGIES FOR PRINCIPALS

Given the impact of group contingencies on planning, deciding, and completing tasks, what strategies can be employed by a school leader in the delegation of decisions and tasks to groups? The following sections outline possible methods for ensuring that groups effectively handle their assignments.

SCHOOL LEADER'S CHECKLIST

School leaders sometimes find it useful to employ a checklist, such as that in Figure 7.2, when considering the delegation of a task or decision to a group.

FIGURE 7.2. CHECKLIST FOR GROUP DELEGATION

The leader has:

___Concluded that the nature of the decision/task is appropriate for group delegation.

___Considered the appropriate size of the group in light of the nature of the task and other factors.

___Insured that the prospective group members understand the decision/task, and understand the parameters within which the decision or task must be completed.

___Determined that group members possess appropriate levels of task maturity, both individually and collectively.

___Weighed the relative merits of a cross-functional team versus a group in which more homogeneous skills and knowledge are present.

___Matched the nature of the decision/task with appropriate representation of creativity and innovation in the group.

___Considered the working relationships of prospective group members and is satisfied that an appropriate level of cohesiveness can be developed among group members.

___Provided sufficient time and other resources to support the effective work of the group.

___Anticipated the potential for groupthink and its consequences, and taken steps to prevent the negative impact of groupthink.

BRAINSTORMING

The techniques associated with brainstorming are widely known. This familiar group process invites members of a group engaged in decision making and task completion to contribute their ideas and suggestions to the process. Various methods of participating exist: some brainstorming techniques call for voluntary participation of individuals; others invite participation in sequence until all members have been heard. Contributions from group members are usually recorded, often on chart paper, marker board, or in some other manner.

The brainstorming technique is a valuable one for creatively generating ideas and prompting broad participation among group members. Additional steps are required to actually generate a strategy for the group to pursue in fulfilling its task or decision. Figure 7.3 outlines the steps in one brainstorming technique.

AFFINITY PROCESS

Groups encounter problems when one or more members assume dominant roles. Administrators who participate in group processes often impact the candor of the group, and unwittingly restrict the flow of ideas, especially if they are inclined to assert their own perspectives early in the discussion (Leana, 1985). There are also the multiple potential risks associated with groupthink.

Affinity process is a technique that is used to combat such problems in group decision-making and task implementation. An affinity process is similar in some ways to brainstorming. It requires that group members generate suggestions to make a decision, solve a problem, or complete some portion of a task. However, because individuals generate their contributions on notepaper, the process has the added benefit of anonymity. This sometimes prompts more reticent members to participate, and may help keep an overzealous group leader or member from dominating the dialogue. The anonymity of the process also helps to preserve confidentiality, and may prompt more candid contributions.

Figure 7.4 outlines the steps for an affinity process. Note that many of the steps are similar to brainstorming. However, this

FIGURE 7.3. BRAINSTORMING: A GROUP PROCESS

Step 1 Clarify the part of the group's task or decision that needs resolution.

Step 2 Invite group members to make suggestions and offer strategies regarding the issue being addressed. This can be managed in several ways. Group members can simply volunteer a response as desired. Every group member might be called upon as the group leader goes about the table. Individuals can pass and be called upon later.

Step 3 Record each response or suggestion on chart paper or marker board so that it is visible to the entire group.

Avoid editing, analyzing or evaluating the contributions of individuals during these first phases of the process.

Step 4 As a group, analyze and try to predict the consequences, both positive and negative, of the various proposed strategies. Bring data, research, and other helpful information to bear on this part of the process.

Step 5 As a group, try to reach consensus on a high quality decision or course of action. If this is not possible, it may be worthwhile to revisit some of the previous steps. If resolution is still not possible, it may be worthwhile to bring in a facilitator.

Step 6 Implement the decision or strategy.

Step 7 Evaluate the quality of the group's work as results become available. Factor such results into related future brainstorming, decision-making and task-completion efforts.

FIGURE 7.4. AFFINITY PROCESS

Step 1 Clarify the part of the group's task or decision that needs resolution. For example, a committee might be tasked to come up with strategies for making the school environment safer and less disruptive. The particular part of the task might be for the group to identify safety and orderliness issues needing the most immediate attention.

Step 2 Invite group members to silently write suggestions and strategies regarding the issue being addressed. A useful way to manage this part of the process is to have members generate their ideas on small pieces of adhesive note paper. As they write the ideas, have them stick the individual notes on a large piece of chart or poster paper. Encourage members to look at the ideas of others as they are placing their own on the chart paper—they may stimulate new ideas!

Step 3 Continuing to work in silence, have group members group the ideas into any categories. The members will merely move the pieces of note paper about the chart paper into groups of similar ideas that appear evident to them.

Step 4 Open the process up for discussion by labeling the categories. Using the school safety scenario from Step 1, the group might see patterns in the responses that would be labeled hallway behavior during class changes, tardiness and attendance, conduct in the cafeteria, visitor access to the building, etc. As discussion takes place, some additional arranging of the ideas may occur. The goal of this step is to synthesize and categorize the contributions of individuals.

As with brainstorming, avoid editing, analyzing, or evaluating the contributions of individuals during these first phases of the process.

Step 5 As a group, analyze and try to prioritize the areas of concern. Bring data, research, and other helpful information to bear on this part of the process.

Complete the affinity process using steps 5–7 from the brainstorming process in Figure 7.3.

process has the additional benefit of allowing the group to graphically organize member input in order to synthesize and systematize the contributions.

TOOLS TO FACILITATE GROUP DECISION MAKING AND TASK COMPLETION

GROUP FACILITATOR

Groups often find it difficult to work together on complex or important decisions and tasks, particularly if they have little training in group processes and group dynamics. A trained facilitator can aid groups in organizing themselves and completing their work. An outside facilitator can often be more objective and can help to insure that dominant personalities don't monopolize discussion and decision-making processes.

In addition to helping groups organize and complete projects, a facilitator can also use the group's time and work together as an opportunity to build understanding of group dynamics and skill in group processes. This strengthens the group's prospects for ongoing success in decision making and task completion. The experience in such groups can also serve as training that will enable members to become facilitators for other groups.

A final benefit of using a facilitator is the opportunity that such an individual provides a formal leader, such as a school administrator, to assume a participant role. This usually results in less directive leader behavior, and more objective processing of decisions and tasks. As noted in the section on groupthink, greater neutrality and less directive leader behavior can prompt more active involvement and creativity from other members.

TECHNOLOGY

Miranda (1994) and others have become increasingly interested in the value of technology as a support mechanism for group processes. Video technology affords opportunities for group members and outside participants (experts or stakeholders, for example) to participate in the group when they can not be physically present.

Networked computer terminals can facilitate brainstorming, affinity processes, and other generative group activities. The assurance of anonymity and simultaneous input that such technology provides helps group members to avoid normative influences which might serve to stifle ideas and creative solutions. Such technology can also expedite information processing such as synthesizing ideas, tallying responses, and providing for rapid processes related to sorting, searching, and tabulating information. An ongoing record of the group's work is greatly facilitated by such technology.

CODE OF CONDUCT

Group work frequently produces conflict. After all, individuals have their own ideas, opinions, preferences, and vested interests. Conflict is likely—indeed, it is desirable. Our previous analysis of the groupthink phenomenon points to the potential negative consequences for groups that do not experience at least some level of disagreement.

A written code of conduct can help to maximize the work of a group by elaborating formally the group members' expectations of one another, by focusing individuals on the positive elements of conflict, and by specifying unwanted behaviors. Because a group's code of conduct works best when it has been developed and agreed upon by the members themselves, there isn't a particular recipe for such codes. Figure 7.5, however, describes the elements included in one school team's code of conduct as an illustration of one group's expectations for its members in carrying out their work together.

APPLYING YOUR KNOWLEDGE

1. The administration and faculty of Santa Clara Middle School are excited. The county commissioners have approved the construction of a new facility to replace their aging school. The superintendent and principal agree that the staff, along with parent representatives, should be actively involved in the planning of the new buildings and interior spaces.

FIGURE 7.5. NEWTON-HANOVER HIGH SCHOOL
TEAM OPERATING PROCEDURES

♦ Team Leader Commitments:

- Confirms and announces the meeting times and locations.

- Makes sure that any supplies needed for the meeting are available.

- Assures that an agenda is available.

- Reviews agenda topics and meeting objectives at the beginning of the meeting. Topics are usually generated at the previous meeting; additional topics and/or adjustments to the agenda are discussed and agreed upon by the team at the beginning of the meeting.

- Assigns a timekeeper at the beginning of the meeting to keep things on schedule.

- Assigns a recorder to keep the minutes of team sessions. Provides status reports to team members and others as needed.

- Helps team members evaluate their work and progress, meeting by meeting.

♦ Member Commitments:

- Attends meetings, and is on time.

- Listens to others, and allows them to finish their thoughts.

- Offers opinions, handles disagreements with courtesy and professionalism.

- Limits discussion to the agenda topics at hand.

- Honors the team's confidentiality with regard to sensitive issues.

- Supports the team's decisions, or seeks to resolve differences in professional manner within the team.

- Follows through on tasks, obligations, and assignments from the team.

Differences of opinion are already evident in many areas of the planning process. Some teachers want classrooms arranged in groups of four that will accommodate team teaching, in order to place a math, language arts, social studies, and science teachers adjacent to one another to serve the same group of students. Several of the science teachers think it would be better to have a separate science department in order to be more efficient, and to create specialized science learning areas that can be used by all students and science teachers, rather than the generic sort of classroom that would probably have to be built for the team plan.

Visual and performing arts teachers are already concerned that their disciplines will not receive adequate instructional space. The principal anticipates a disagreement over whether to focus on computers in every classroom, or to focus on setting up additional computer labs. There is even a debate over whether to have the cafeteria set up with traditional serving lines or arranged more like a food court at a shopping mall.

With classmates or colleagues discuss the responsibilities of various committees that might be formed. Review the group contingencies addressed in this chapter as you consider factors the superintendent and principal should weigh in assigning individuals to committees. What, if any, preparatory training or discussions would the committees need to undertake prior to beginning their work?

2. The administration of Barden High School is interested in moving from a traditional six-period class schedule to a block schedule. There has been some preliminary discussion with faculty and parents. There is sufficient interest to warrant more serious consideration of such a change. Much has to be done, including researching the relative benefits of various scheduling models. Assuming that such

research prompts an adoption of the block schedule model, additional effort must be undertaken to plan, communicate, and implement the transition to the new schedule.

What types of teams should be formed to participate in the investigation and decision-making processes related to adopting a new schedule? Which variables should be considered in assigning members to the teams? What background information, training, and commitments, if any, will be necessary for team members? In what ways, and when, might cross-functional teams be valuable to the investigation and decision-making processes?

Assume that the investigation leads to a consensus to adopt the block schedule. How would you respond to the questions in the preceding paragraph as they relate to planning, communicating, and implementing the new schedule?

EXTENDING YOUR KNOWLEDGE

The literature on group dynamics and group processes in organizations is extensive. To enhance your knowledge, conduct a literature review using these descriptors:

- Group dynamics
- Group processes
- Facilitative leadership
- Groupthink
- Quality control teams
- Cross-categorical teaming

Take time to explore materials on these topics. Using this information, modify the resource materials from the chapter to make them more useful in your particular circumstances.

8

TIME AND RESOURCE CONTINGENCIES AND THEIR EFFECT ON DELEGATION

SETTING THE STAGE

THE SITUATION

Andre Daniel has been principal of Kingsport School, a large pre-kindergarten through eighth grade school, for 16 years. A new middle school has been built in a nearby community, and the county's board of education has determined that all sixth, seventh, and eighth graders will attend the new school. The resulting loss of students will reduce the number of buses available to the Kingsport attendance area, and will necessitate a complete reconfiguration of bus routes and pupil assignment to buses.

Early in his tenure at Kingsport School, Andre developed bus routes that have remained virtually intact since their creation. Responsibility for the routes has belonged to Andre because he has preferred to manage this task entirely on his own.

Immediately following the end of the school year prior to the transfer of the sixth through eighth graders, Andre begins the process of reconfiguring the bus routes. He has scarcely begun the task, however, before he becomes ill. He makes an effort to carry out his duties, including drafting the new bus routes, but as he grows increasingly weak, a number of things remain undone. At midsummer, Andre's doctor confines him to bed rest, and a number of duties, including the responsibility for re-designing the transportation routes, are delegated to Jason Beasley, a newly hired and largely inexperienced assistant principal.

Jason is provided with the work done to date, which consists of no more than three pages of notes and a few hastily sketched tentative routes. With four weeks remaining until the students return for the new school year, he sets out to complete the process. He spends hours each week driving around the district, calling parents, and drawing routes by hand. The task is overwhelming and Jason runs into complication after complication. Finally, just days before the first day of school for students, he calls a meeting of the bus drivers still assigned to Kingsport.

The meeting is disjointed, with drivers expressing concerns about the viability of the proposed routes. They are also concerned about the inequity of driving time and, thus, the earning potential for some drivers. Jason becomes frustrated and finally concludes the meeting with the request that the drivers begin the year under the new routes, and with a promise that he will make adjustments to the plan as necessary.

Drivers arrive to pick up their buses on the afternoon prior to the opening day of school. Several drivers, primarily those whose routes are disproportionately short, fail to report. Jason sends out a desperate plea for substitutes, but is unable to send out three of the buses. The first day of school is a fiasco for Kingsport's transportation system, with irregular arrivals at student pickup points, a number of children left at stops, and a flood of irate phone calls to Jason, the county superintendent's office, and to school board members.

YOUR THOUGHTS ARE?

Consider the circumstances in which the responsibility for the development of the new bus routes was assigned to Jason. Previous chapters on leader, task, individual, and group contingencies should provide some insights into the causes of the poor performance of the transportation system on opening day. But there are other contingencies that help explain Jason's dilemma as well. Additional contingencies include the resources available to an individual(s) to facilitate the completion of assigned tasks. With colleagues or classmates, identify the resources that might have helped Jason to better fulfill his responsibility for creating the new bus routes.

INTRODUCTION

Previous chapters explored the relationship between delegation and leader, task, individual, and group contingencies. These are important considerations in decision making and delegation. However, even in circumstances where the leader possesses excellent delegation skills and the match between tasks and individuals/groups is appropriate, additional contingencies must be considered, including the availability of time and other important resources for accomplishing the tasks, roles, and responsibilities that have been assigned.

This chapter explores resource contingencies. The next section is an overview of literature related to resource issues in delegation and decision making. It is followed by sections that provide practical suggestions for factoring resource contingencies into delegation processes.

SELECTED RESOURCE CONTINGENCIES AND DELEGATION

The definition of tasks/roles, and the identification of individuals/groups to carry them out are certainly critical leadership skills. However, effective delegation requires more than the ability to match people and work activities, and goes beyond a willingness to share authority. In a keynote address to workforce development conference participants, Hertz noted, "Empowerment is more than collaboration—it's providing the right tools and resources" (November 3, 1997). The individuals must have the resources to see assignments through to completion. White (1974) lists work-related resources as skills, knowledge, money, materials, equipment, customers, patients, and clients.

Blase and Kirby (1992) identify four types of resources that are necessary to enable school staff members to fulfill tasks and responsibilities:

- Financial resources: financial resources include obvious expenditures such as project funding, materials, and supplies. Fiscal resources can also include costs such as substitute teacher salaries, which free staff members to complete assignments.

- Facilities: such resources include physical space, equipment, telep:.ones, and special technology necessary to fulfill responsibilities.

- Professional development: as observed in Chapters 6 and 7 regarding individual and group contingencies, assignments vary in complexity and the related need for participan⁺ expertise. When the expertise to fulfill certain assignments is not present, or the persons with such expertise are otherwise occupied, building such skills is necessary, and the costs of professional development become another resource contingency.

- Time: time is a critical variable in the fulfillment of tasks. Staff members need the opportunity to meet, to plan, to resolve problems, and to carry out delegated decisions, tasks, roles, and responsibilities. In addition, some assignments/roles are more time-consuming than others. Groups typically require more time than individuals to carry out some parts of the decision-making and task completion processes (Hoy & Miskel, 1991). In addition, some tasks are more urgent than others. The level of crisis attached to some tasks/roles may place the resource of time in relatively short supply.

Other resources are necessary for task completion, as well. Adequate information and data pertinent to delegated duties are essential for effective performance. Leaders have a responsibility to insure that such resources are available, or that delegatees have the means to seek out such information resources. Ironically, in school environments, those who are arguably most in need of such resources—young and/or inexperienced teachers—are often least likely to receive priority attention from those in leadership (Blase & Kirby, 1992).

The availability and use of resources influences behavior in organizations. In work settings that employ collaborative decision-making, individuals and groups often seek to induce one another to modify or relinquish their control of resources (White, 1974). White further contends that organizational goals may be realized by collaborative decision-making regarding the allocation of resources. He observes that work groups are generally more cohesive when their resources are not divisible. The accessibility of resources and the discretion over the use of resources enhances an individual or group's sense of empowerment, and expands the range of alternatives an individual/group will bring to bear on a given task.

Resource contingencies associated with decision making and delegation include the:

- Accessibility of resources of finance, facilities, professional development, time, and information;
- Collaborative management of resources;
- Divisibility of resources; and
- Discretion of individuals/groups over the deployment of resources.

Clearly, the availability of appropriate and adequate resources is a powerful delegation contingency. The practical implications of resource deployment for delegation decisions are discussed next.

FIGHTING THE RESOURCE BATTLE

Providing the resources necessary to enable staff members to make quality decisions and to effectively complete tasks is more than just a practical issue; it is also an issue of ethics. Members of the organization are frequently evaluated on the basis of their effectiveness in completing assignments and projects, whether as individuals or as members of a group. Such evaluations are fair only when individuals are given reasonable access to the time and other resources necessary for quality performance. A school's overall effectiveness is a synthesis of the quality of decision-making and task completion by the individuals and groups within the organization. Because such organizational effectiveness reflects on the leadership, a school leader is ill-advised to shortchange staff members on the time and tools they will need when assigned decisions, tasks, and responsibilities.

Resources are rarely deemed sufficient; the notion of resource scarcity is especially prevalent in public sector organizations. A school leader must become skilled in balancing resources across a variety of needs, programs, projects, and emerging priorities. The following sections offer suggestions for dealing with time and the other resources that are necessary for decisions and tasks that are delegated to others.

COLLABORATIVE RESOURCE DEPLOYMENT

School leaders, especially superintendents, and often principals, usually have significant discretion over the assignment of time and material resources. White (1974) reminds us that the organization usually provides safeguards that constrain such leaders from using resources for personal interests. On the other hand, when used optimally, resources have great power to influence and explain organizational behavior. Because of the power of resources to affect the attainment of individual work related tasks, and overarching organizational goals, it is wise to engage the organization's members in decisions regarding the use and deployment of such resources.

CREATING RESERVES

The process of deploying resources is of critical importance. Judging needs across programs and projects requires skill, judgment, and (as we have already noted) the collective wisdom of the stakeholders in the organization. However, even under the best of circumstances, some resource needs may be underestimated, and new needs, projects, and assignments may arise during the course of the budget cycle. It is wise to create reserves to address the needs that arise during the course of the year. Delegation of new projects and assignments is made easier when there are potential resources to call on.

REDUCING SCOPE/EXTENDING TIME/ADDING PEOPLE

Delegated tasks and decisions need to be accompanied by sufficient time to insure a quality product. The time needed should, ideally, be determined jointly by the leader and the delegatee. This provides the staff member with the opportunity to balance the new assignment against existing responsibilities.

When disagreements occur over the time needed, or when actual experience with the new task suggests that the time allocated is inappropriate, several options exist. Additional time may be allocated. If the task or decision is time sensitive, or particularly urgent, and additional time is not possible, other options exist. The scope of the project may be reduced, additional persons may be called on to assist, or help may be sought from sources outside of the school.

SEEKING ADDITIONAL RESOURCES

School leaders who, along with their colleagues in the school, want to pursue new projects and tasks, may often be frustrated by the limitation of resources which is characteristic of so many public organizations. An effective leader works at finding other ways to secure resources for the tasks the leader wants to delegate to persons in the school.

Reference was made earlier to creating reserves so as to be able to pursue projects and assignments that arise during the course of a fiscal year. Principals should be aware that central office administrators often do the same thing with major budget categories and materials/equipment inventories. In some instances, finding the additional resources for a task or assignment that is to be delegated may be as easy as a request to the central office for some help from such a reserve source.

Grants from governments and foundations are often available for projects; a wise school leader cultivates knowledge of such sources and develops the capacity personally and among staff members to pursue such opportunities. Business and industry often look for ways to be of service in the community, particularly in schools. Opportunities to secure resources for delegated projects may be simply a phone call or visit away.

Some projects need greater time than is available from staff at hand. Volunteers should be sought who can lend a hand in such instances. Naturally, building expertise among such individuals is necessary to insure quality products, but assistance from the community can do much to expand the human resources available when time is not negotiable.

Negotiation

Every leader wants to see important issues decided, and important tasks accomplished in a timely fashion with high-quality results. However, there inevitably are circumstances when a task or decision assigned to an individual or group either does not proceed according to the original timetable or is hindered by a lack of other types of resources.

Naturally, a school leader is called on to make judgments about instances in which a staff member is being unreasonable about his or her concerns regarding time and other resources. But the effective leader will listen carefully to such concerns, and make adjustments whenever possible to assure both high-quality task completion and healthy staff relationships.

In some instances, the pressure for decisions or task completion are compounded by external influences. The superintendent or a board member may be urging rapid response or strict adherence to a particular timetable. Again, the school leader has to make judgments about the progress that staff members are making and the degree of additional pressure that is appropriate for these individuals. But the leader is also called on to advocate for staff when such external pressures are unreasonable. Skill in negotiating with such external entities is essential and should be cultivated by the effective school leader.

It is evident that a number of strategies can guide school leaders in the provision of resources to insure that delegated tasks and decisions are completed effectively. A summary of these strategies is presented in the form of a school leader's checklist (Figure 8.1).

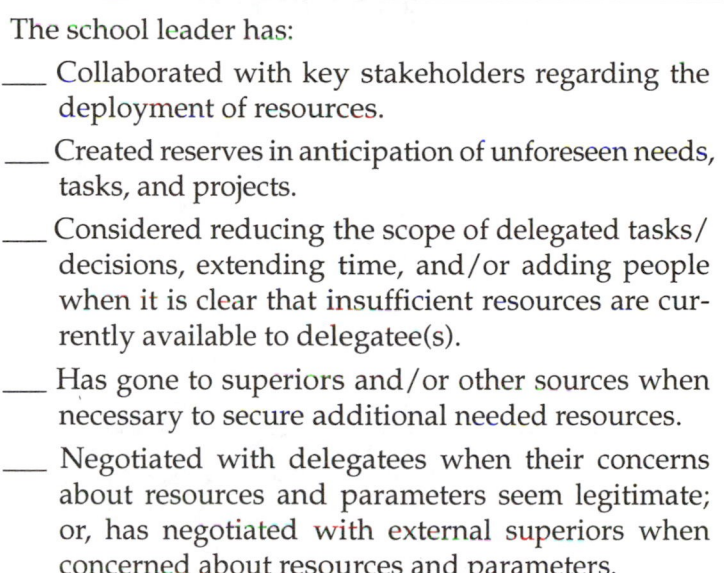

FIGURE 8.1. RESOURCE CONTINGENCIES: A CHECKLIST

The school leader has:

___ Collaborated with key stakeholders regarding the deployment of resources.

___ Created reserves in anticipation of unforeseen needs, tasks, and projects.

___ Considered reducing the scope of delegated tasks/ decisions, extending time, and/or adding people when it is clear that insufficient resources are currently available to delegatee(s).

___ Has gone to superiors and/or other sources when necessary to secure additional needed resources.

___ Negotiated with delegatees when their concerns about resources and parameters seem legitimate; or, has negotiated with external superiors when concerned about resources and parameters.

SUMMARY: A LEADER'S RESPONSE TO RESOURCE CONSTRAINTS

As the preceding sections illustrate, the availability of certain resources impacts the quality of delegation and the degree to which others can truly be empowered in the organization. Figure 8.2 highlights decision-making junctures that are confronted by an administrator as the administrator makes determinations about the resource constraints that may affect certain decisions. While this is only one formula for tying together a complex set of leadership variables, it does summarize the major resource contingencies associated with delegation and decision making. It also suggests courses of action depending upon the leader's assessment of such constraints with regard to key delegation considerations. The model also examines the potential consequences of certain leader decisions.

Figure 8.2. A Leader's Response to Resource Contingencies

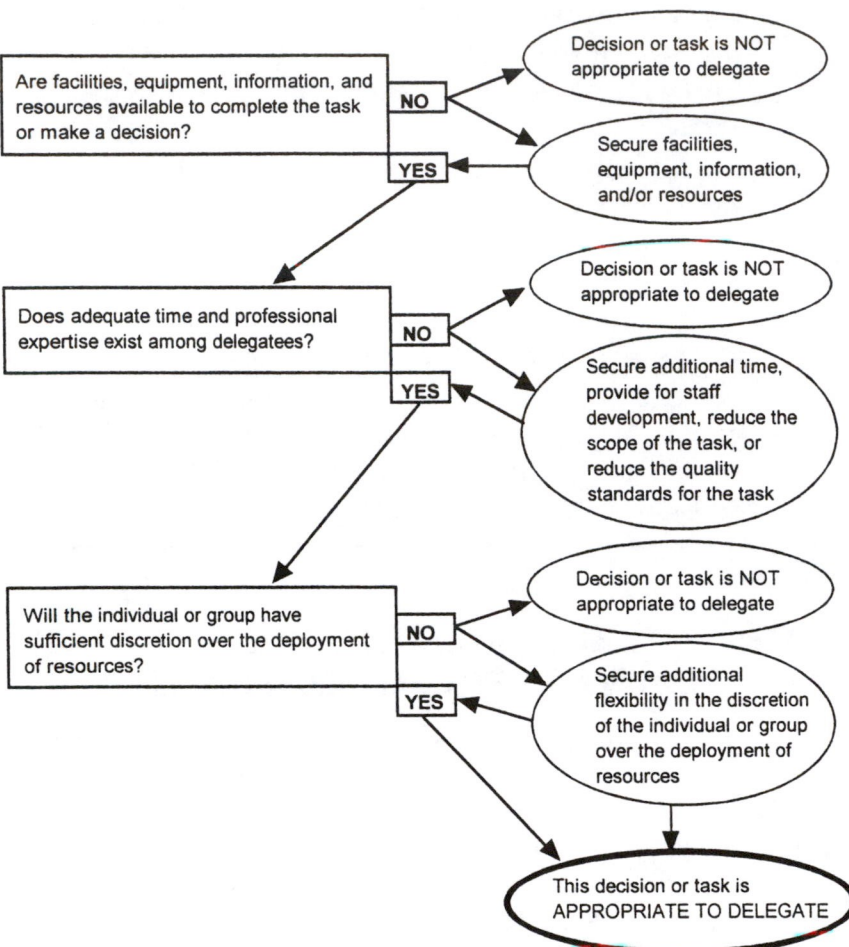

APPLYING YOUR KNOWLEDGE

1. Return to the vignette involving Jason Beasley and the new bus routes at the beginning of this chapter. Having now read the chapter, can you identify additional resources that might have enabled Jason to do a better job of developing the new bus routes? Discuss your conclusions with colleagues or classmates.

2. Consider the following illustrations of staff members participating in decisions regarding the deployment of resources:

   - Principal Julio Herrera of Northern Middle School uses a comprehensive process for resource planning and deployment which begins with faculty and PTA agreement on major goals for the coming school year. New projects and commitments, expansion of materials and equipment in certain areas, and requirements for meeting new mandates are discussed up front, and agreed upon. The staff conducts the budget planning process for each new year by having departments collaboratively build their respective budget requests. A representative from each department, along with parent representatives, then participates in a cross-functional team which works with the principal to consolidate and prioritize the requests for the whole school.

     When the actual allotments for Northern are returned to the school, the cross-functional team returns to the table to examine priorities and resource allocations across the school in light of the final budget figures. Minor adjustments are often made among the top priorities, but only through consensus of the group.

   - Pearlie Eakes is principal of Lincoln High School, and works with 78 faculty members. Scheduling these teachers is a mammoth task. She realizes that the manner in which the resource of each individual's time is used is important not only to the school's functioning, but also of tremendous importance to the individuals themselves. She has, therefore, begun requiring teachers in each department to work together as a team to propose the courses that each will teach and the preferred time slots for teaching and planning. Special assignments and time slots for nonteaching extra duties are factored into the schedule as well.

Staff complaints about schedules and assignments have diminished remarkably from the days when the principal and counselor made scheduling decisions unilaterally. Based on the success of the new process, Pearlie is convinced of the benefits of having the staff help decide upon the effective use of one of its most important resources—its collective time.

With classmates or colleagues, evaluate the pluses and minuses of collaborative decision making regarding the deployment of resources in these two case studies.

9

AUTHORITY/ JURISDICTION CONTINGENCIES AND THEIR EFFECT ON DELEGATION

SETTING THE STAGE

THE SITUATION

Jamie Arrington is the principal of Carver Middle School. She believes that democratic leadership is healthy and has been inclined to give teachers a role in many of the decisions that are made in the school. However, some decisions and tasks are not delegated. These areas, reasons Jamie, are the exclusive domain of the principal, and even though some of the issues are very relevant to staff members, she reserves the authority to make such decisions and carry out such tasks herself.

In some cases, Jamie's reluctance to share authority is the result of policy constraints. In such instances, she perceives that laws or local regulations prevent the inclusion of others. A case in point is the selection of new teachers. Board policy and state law clearly indicate that the school principal shall recommend teacher candidates to the superintendent. The superintendent, in turn, recommends prospective teachers to the board of education, which makes the final decision regarding employment.

In Jamie's mind, the policy clearly precludes delegation of the process and participative decision making. In addition, she sincerely believes that staff members lack the skills and legal knowledge to participate meaningfully in such decisions. She is also of the opinion that staff members will not see the "big picture," which is necessary when balancing an applicant's teaching credentials with, for example, the applicant's ability to coach a major sport. Besides, most applicants are interviewed and approved in the summer, and it would be difficult to bring teachers in from their vacations to participate in the process.

YOUR THOUGHTS ARE?

Analyze Jamie's rationale for excluding participation in staff selection. With others, evaluate the significance of the jurisdictional constraints, specifically the board policy and statute that assign the principal exclusive responsibility for making personnel recommendations to the superintendent. Discuss the course of action that you would recommend Jamie take in response to the concerns that have arisen among staff members.

INTRODUCTION

The opportunity to delegate is impacted by a number of variables. Many of these contingencies were discussed in previous chapters. A final set of contingencies revolves around rules, policies, laws, and personal power constraints imposed by administrators themselves. The appropriateness—even the legality—of delegation is, in some instances, constrained by such variables, which we call authority contingencies.

This chapter provides a brief examination of the literature related to authority parameters. An additional section offers suggestions and guides to school leaders as they consider the impact of such parameters on effective delegation.

SELECTED AUTHORITY CONTINGENCIES AND DELEGATION

WHY WAIT UNTIL NOW TO DISCUSS AUTHORITY CONTINGENCIES?

It may seem inappropriate to reserve a discussion of authority contingencies, which may be nonnegotiable, to such a late section of the text. An examination of other contingencies affecting delegation would appear meaningless if the authority to delegate is constrained or forbidden by policy or law. A case in point might be the previously mentioned process by which a school district's new teachers are selected. To consider delegation appears pointless in such instances; weighing contingencies such as expertise, time, and other resource contingencies is apparently meaningless. With this in mind, it seems that authority contingencies should be the first focus of attention, and no other contingencies are relevant if authority to share decisions and delegate responsibilities is constrained.

It is perhaps too easy to fall back on the assumption that the rules prevent participation. Indeed, raising authority constraints is often a subterfuge for a leader's reluctance to empower others. It is for this reason that the discussion of authority contingencies is reserved for this place in the text. A wise administrator will think creatively about the inclusion of organization members in decisions and decision implementation.

Consider the scenario involving the selection of teachers in Setting the Stage. While the legal constraints for the final selection of teachers cannot be ignored, a creative administrator may find a number of meaningful opportunities for member involvement in the process. As always, depending upon individual, group, and resource contingencies, the principal wants to make thoughtful judgments about such participation.

ASSIGNING AUTHORITY

Authority contingencies do not apply only to the latitude available to the administrator in determining whether or not a decision or task can be delegated. They are also a major consideration in the principal's decisions about *how much* jurisdiction a delegatee will be given over the decision or task.

Using the teacher-selection scenario described previously, the school administrator who believes in empowerment might invite staff participation in the process of hiring new teachers in ways that do not violate pertinent laws or policies. Such authority lies on a continuum between full authority and fulfilling an advisory role. Gradations in this continuum are reflected in the delegation hierarchy shown in Figure 9.1.

COAXING OUT FLEXIBILITY: THE TREND TOWARD WAIVERS

Increasingly, states are disposed to lessen regulatory constraints upon schools. The trend toward local control and site-based management has prompted legislatures and state boards of education to be less rigid with policies. Often, the quid pro quo for such flexibility is greater accountability, or heightened expectations for the actual performance results. While some easing of regulatory constraint is codified, it is often necessary to seek some types of flexibility through a waiver process. Such processes allow local schools and districts to apply for waivers on such polices as class size requirements, converting funds for teaching positions to other uses, and vice versa.

DISCLOSING PARAMETERS IN ADVANCE

The nature of the participation and the amount of authority delegated when individuals are assigned a decision or task to complete are particularly important considerations. Taylor and Card (1985) caution that administrators risk the trust of staff members if they have perceptions of the discretion available to delegatees that differ from the perceptions of the staff members themselves. If the delegated authority available in the selection of new teachers, for example, is limited to a review of résumés and advice about preferred candidates, the administrator is wise to make such parameters, known in advance. Arriving at the point of a decision on the new staff member, and only then learning that the principal has reserved the final decision, can be a source of great frustration to staff members.

FIGURE 9.1. A HIERARCHY OR PARTICIPANT AUTHORITY

Level 1: The leader makes decisions and performs tasks without assigning authority to others:

Level 2: The leader provides others the authority to offer advice and opinions. The leader retains the authority to make decisions and/or perform tasks:

Level 3: The leader shares authority as a member of a group which generates decisions and performs tasks: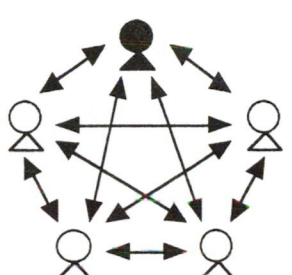

Level 4: The leader assigns the authority for making decisions and performing tasks to individuals or groups: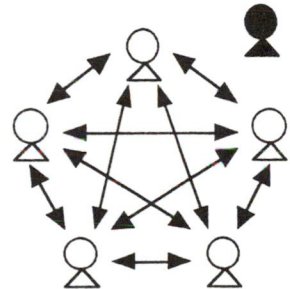

A WORD ABOUT COLLECTIVE BARGAINING

Collective bargaining and union contract agreements affect a leader's discretion in response to authority parameters. Some authors have noted that unionization has often constrained school-based decision making and increased the extent of centralized decision making (Kelley & Rodriguez, 1977; Kerchner,

1979). Others, such as Baldwin (1990), have noted that the participation of staff members in strategic decision-making raises questions regarding their role. Does such participation confer management status upon them? What are the implications of such status in the contract negotiating process?

Contracts often have specific provisions governing a school leader's discretion in delegating decisions, tasks, and responsibilities. Likewise, the amount of authority available to leaders and union members respectively may be tightly constrained for various decision making and delegation circumstances. The effective leader will understand such constraints, and, more importantly, will not allow such constraints to limit participation and delegation any more than is necessary.

SUMMARY: A LEADER'S RESPONSE TO AUTHORITY CONSTRAINTS

Obviously, authority contingencies are significant considerations in the process of deciding which decisions/tasks will be delegated, and the level of responsibility that will be assigned to delegatees. Authority contingencies include:

- The rigidity of authority constraints;
- The inclination of the leader toward prior disclosure of authority parameters;
- The leader's disposition toward policy flexibility;
- Constraints in collective bargaining agreements.

Thoughtful consideration of such contingencies, provision of opportunities for involvement within the confines of such parameters, and mutual understanding of the limits of participation in advance will serve a leader well in the process of delegation.

Figure 9.2 highlights decision-making junctures that are confronted as an administrator makes determinations about the authority constraints that may affect certain decisions. While this is only one formula for tying together a complex set of leadership variables, it does summarize the major authority contingencies associated with delegation and decision making. It also suggests courses of action depending upon the leader's assess

Figure 9.2. Authority Contingencies: A Leader's Response

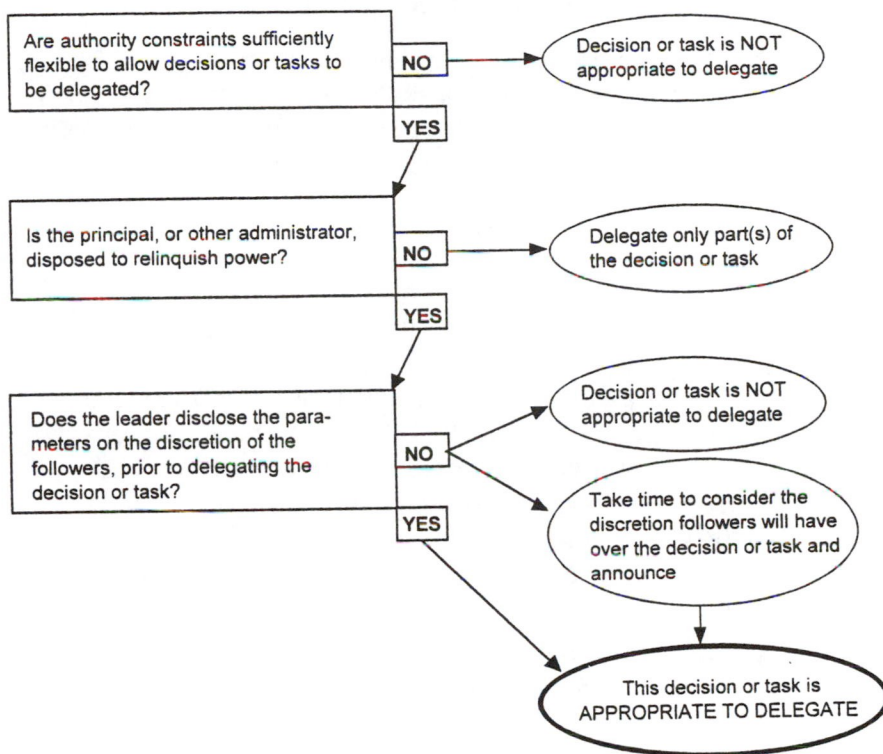

ment of such constraints. The model also examines the potential consequences of certain leader decisions.

APPLYING YOUR KNOWLEDGE

Consider the following vignettes. In what ways might authority or jurisdictional constraints limit the discretion of participants in the decision or task? What can the principal or administrator do to minimize the negative impact of these constraints?

- ♦ Principal Joni Meier has assigned the social studies department the task of revising the guides for teaching about religion in the middle school curriculum. Members of the department are congenial, and have the reputation for never getting into arguments. Knowing the sensitive nature of the assignment she is delegating, what factors should the principal consider as she assigns the task to the group? What advice should she give the department chair, as well as the group, regarding the manner in which they are to proceed? What parameters should she discuss with the group before they begin their work?

- ♦ You are principal of a middle school. New OSHA regulations for electrical safety in career exploration labs have been developed. The district's maintenance director sends the regulations to you. How will you insure compliance with these new codes?

- ♦ You are principal of a large high school. There is a vacant teaching position in the science department. You also have a need to hire a new head football coach, and this is the only faculty vacancy that you are anticipating between now and the beginning of football season. Describe the individuals who might be invited to participate in the process that will be used to fill the science vacancy. What kinds of constraints will be imposed upon their participation and the manner in which they participate?

10

EFFECTIVE DELEGATION AND EMPOWERMENT: PULLING THE PIECES TOGETHER

By now it should be clear that a number of contingencies affect the propensity of school leaders to delegate and to empower others. This chapter examines the interaction of delegation contingencies and offers prescriptions for effective empowerment with all the delegation contingencies in mind.

CONTINGENCIES AFFECTING DELEGATION AND EMPOWERMENT: A RECAP

Consider all that was examined in each of the previous chapters. In Chapter 1, the constructs of delegation and empowerment were introduced. Delegated tasks were distinguished from routine or ongoing responsibilities that are parts of job descriptions or the ordinary duties associated with a certain position in the school organization. The varying motivations of leaders to delegate and empower others were considered.

In Chapter 2, the growing complexity of school leadership was acknowledged. The relationship of delegation and empowerment to contemporary leadership issues was addressed. We suggested ways that a principal's skills and knowledge vis-à-vis delegation and empowerment might influence the principal's overall effectiveness.

Chapter 3 surveyed literature, research, theories, and models that inform dialogues about delegation and empowerment, and that provide a basis for prescribing effective leader behaviors relative to these dimensions of leadership. Based on this literature, a typology of contingencies associated with delegation and empowerment was proposed. Chapters 4 thru 9 examined each category of variables.

Chapter 4 explored ways in which the knowledge, skills, and perspectives of leaders are related to delegation. The varying nature of tasks and the impact of this variation on delegation were explored in Chapter 5. Chapters 6 and 7 examined the variables that affect the readiness, willingness, and the ability of individuals and groups to manage delegated decisions and tasks. In Chapter 8, the impact of time and resources on the successful completion of delegated tasks was considered. Chapter 9 concluded the examination of contingencies associated with delegation by exploring the potential limits that authority and jurisdictional constraints can impose upon empowerment decisions.

Although we have examined these contingency categories separately for ease of understanding, these variables interact in complex ways to impact the effectiveness of delegation. How should a school leader juggle these multiple variables as they determine which decisions and tasks are to be delegated?

FIRST, USE THE ORGANIZATION'S VISION AND GOALS AS AN ANCHOR FOR DELEGATION AND EMPOWERMENT

Delegation and empowerment can be powerful in the management of a school. However, such processes engage multiple individuals with multiple perspectives and multiple interpretations regarding decisions to be made and work to be done. In such circumstances, there is the potential that delegated decisions and tasks may move in directions that are unintended.

High-quality results can be produced through a participative process, but something more than leader-group collaboration is required of administrators in such complex management environments. The leader could tightly oversee the decision-making and implementation process, but such behaviors should be reserved for circumstances in which participants demonstrate low task maturity. If such micromanagement is routinely necessary, there may be little point to delegating the tasks. How then, can a principal or other school leader ensure that the processes of delegation and empowerment produce results that are aligned with the organization's aims?

The answer is straightforward, although not simple. A clear organizational vision helps to provide an anchor for organizational behavior. Indeed, Peters and Waterman (1982) contend that a clear sense of mission is essential to organizational effectiveness. Goals that articulate the aims associated with the vision provide additional guidance. Specific strategies and evaluation measures assist in describing how the vision is to be accomplished and also serve to help align activity in the school. It is also helpful to engage the staff and community in a deliberate and inclusive process of defining the vision and ultimately the beliefs and values derived from it. These processes help guide participant behavior.

Visioning and goal-setting processes will not, by themselves, assure aligned behavior in an organization that embraces delegation and empowerment. However, these processes can contribute mightily to a shared understanding of the directions in which decisions and tasks should go.

Second, Tie It All Together

To lead effectively, administrators must understand the contingencies that affect delegation and empowerment. It is also critical to begin with the end in mind. Understanding the interrelationship of the contingencies and giving structure to the leadership behaviors associated with delegation is the next important step. Muse et al. (1993) provide a particularly useful outline of necessary steps in an effective delegation process. An adaptation of the steps and sequence in the process follows.

1. Define the decision or task to be completed.

    Much has been said previously of the importance of clarifying decisions and tasks that are to be completed. Likewise, disclosing parameters, assessing the potential risks, and evaluating the complexity of the decision or task is important at this stage.

Chapter 5 further explicates prerequisites for defining and clarifying the task.

2. Identify those to whom the decision or task might be assigned.

This step involves assessing the task maturity, conceptual complexity, and motivation of those to whom the decision or task may be assigned. An individual or team may be chosen for the task, and Chapters 6 and 7 provide insights into such selection processes.

3. Announce the assignment of those who will be carrying out the decision or task (McCall, 1994).

This step is often neglected in the process, yet it is important. Making others aware of the assignment of a task to an individual or group accomplishes several things. When this happens, an individual needing information about the decision or task is spared the time that might otherwise be wasted by inquiring in the wrong place. This also saves time for the administrator who might otherwise have been the source to whom the inquiry was directed. The administrator then assumes the dual role of facilitating the interaction and the mutual understanding of the delegatee(s) and the school organization (Finch, 1977). The announcement also provides status to the delegatee(s) and helps to legitimize the requests that they might make of others whose assistance is needed in fulfilling the task.

4. Assign responsibility to prospective delegates.

Delegating decisions and tasks also implies relinquishing jurisdiction and assigning responsibility to others. Providing adequate and appropriate discretion to delegatees is important, just as disclosing constraints on their discretion is essential. Chapter 9 examines the issues related to this step in the delegation and empowerment process.

5. Provide support, autonomy, and feedback as needed for those assigned to the decision or task.

Support includes resources, advice, and monitoring. Autonomy is also necessary, both as an indication of the trust the administrator holds in the delegatee(s), and to make efficient use of the administrator's time. The degree of autonomy, direction, and monitoring provided to those responsible for the decision or task is likely to vary according to their task maturity, conceptual complexity, and motivation. Chapter 8 provides insights into resource contingencies, and Chapter 6 examines the issues of guidance, oversight, and autonomy for delegatee(s).

6. Focus leadership on accountability for results.

As a general rule, the principal will want to concentrate more on product and less on process, whether followup is at specific intervals or at the completion of the task. However, theories of situational leadership suggest that the leader must also be skilled at understanding when to stand back, when to facilitate, when to oversee, and, yes, even when to interfere. Blase and Kirby (1992) suggest that "gentle nudges" such as offering advice, alternatives, and options may be appreciated even by more task mature delegatees. There may also be occasions when the principal must assert leadership to deal with an individual or group member who is serving to obstruct progress, or even to sabotage an assignment. Chapters 4 and 6 explore leadership behaviors and participant contingencies in which each of these leadership behaviors is appropriate.

7. Assess performance and results.

While the importance of evaluating the outcomes of delegated tasks would appear to be self-evident, such assessment is often neglected. Building in the time for evaluation of delegation processes and results is an important element of organizational accountability, and it provides insights with which to improve the effectiveness of future empowerment processes. The next section of this chapter explores the assessment process in greater detail.

These steps offer a useful procedure for delegation and the empowerment of others. Together, they provide a basis for linking the various delegation contingencies examined in earlier chapters. Perhaps most useful, the steps synthesize the prescriptions for effective delegation that have been explored elsewhere in the text. While the model is not intended to be rigid, it does provide a reasonable structure by which a principal can lead the processes of delegation and empowerment. Figure 10.1 provides a graphic summary of the model.

FIGURE 10.1. DELEGATION PROCESS STEPS
(ADAPTED FROM MUSE ET AL., 1993)

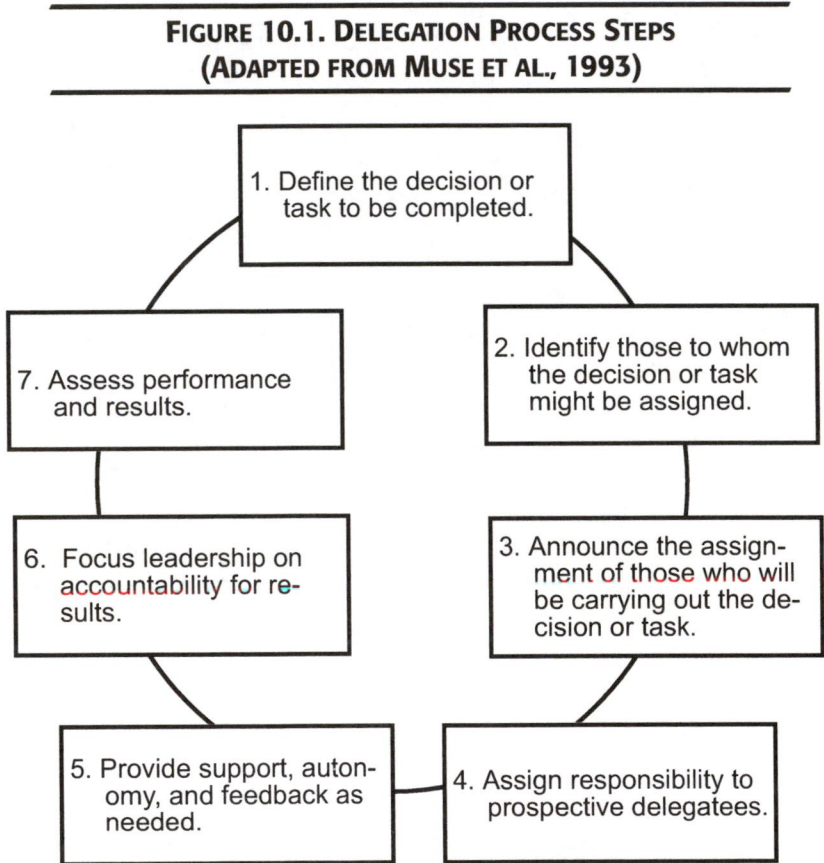

1. Define the decision or task to be completed.

2. Identify those to whom the decision or task might be assigned.

3. Announce the assignment of those who will be carrying out the decision or task.

4. Assign responsibility to prospective delegatees.

5. Provide support, autonomy, and feedback as needed.

6. Focus leadership on accountability for results.

7. Assess performance and results.

THIRD, EVALUATE RESULTS

It seems self-evident that leaders and participants are interested in the quality of results obtained when decisions and tasks are delegated. In spite of this, systematic evaluation and followup rarely occur in any formal manner. Exhaustive followup may be impractical, especially when tasks are either of relatively low consequence, or are unlikely to be repeated. However, it is useful to evaluate the process and results of delegation. This can provide insights into the degree of success realized and guide future related tasks.

PERFORMANCE RESULTS

The previous chapters outlined contingencies related to effective delegation. These variables offer criteria that can be used as a basis for evaluating the delegation process and results. At a minimum, these criteria should provide insights into the performance and dispositions of the leader and the individual delegatee or group. It is also useful to consider the degree to which resources were adequate to support successful completion of the task. Ultimately, the quality of the delegation product is of paramount importance.

At minimum, the leadership criteria associated with the evaluation of a delegated task or decision should include the leader's effectiveness in defining the task, disclosing parameters, supporting participants, and appropriately monitoring progress. In considering the performance of the individual(s) assigned to the task, it is worthwhile to review participant expertise, motivation, and quality of contribution.

Groups should be appraised with some of the same criteria used for individuals, including the task-maturity of the group, as well as the expertise, creativity, and cohesiveness of group members. Also consider any evidence of dysfunctions associated with the groupthink phenomenon discussed in Chapter 7. Finally, weigh whether the number of individuals assigned to the group or team was appropriate for the task.

Evaluating the adequacy of resources as a basis for determining the quality of delegation results is particularly useful. The resource categories evaluated should include time, funds, facilities, and equipment. The adequacy of information and professional development to support quality performance should also be appraised.

The preceding paragraphs recap the *process inputs* associated with delegating decisions and tasks. This is the first of two essential components of evaluation and followup. The second is the quality of the *work product*. Thus, assessing delegation effectiveness requires the appraisal of the decision process and of the task results.

A word of caution is in order here. Being overly critical or exacting in the review of results may have a negative impact upon the future motivation of participants. Thomas (1989) suggests that unless the results are a disaster, the products of delegated decisions and tasks should be accepted as they are. While this is perhaps too relaxed an evaluation posture, leaders who delegate decisions and tasks should recognize that others will sometimes generate solutions and results which differ from those which they might have designed themselves.

Figure 10.2 synthesizes the appraisal criteria outlined in this section. The form can be used by the principal and participants to guide both the planning and evaluation of delegated tasks. Such appraisals should be conducted at initial stages, as well as at the conclusion of the task or decision. They may also be useful at interim stages, especially if all is not proceeding well.

SCHOOL ENVIRONMENT OUTCOMES

As the preceding section suggests, it is important to evaluate the quality of delegated decisions and tasks. It is also helpful to evaluate the degree to which delegation and empowerment have an impact on the quality of the school's overall environment.

Barth (1987) asserts that the impact of effective empowerment activities is to move from the solitary authority of the principal to the collective authority of the members of the school community. Among other benefits to the environment, he contends that the participation of a community of leaders helps to reduce the sense of isolation that often characterizes a setting in which teacher activities are so often confined to their own classrooms. The inclusion of staff and community members in decisions and tasks sends a strong signal to students and to the rest

FIGURE 10.2. EVALUATION OF DELEGATION DECISIONS AND RESULTS

Decision/Task To Be Evaluated _____   Dates: _____ Planning
                                                          _____ Interim Appraisal
Participants _____   _____ Final Appraisal

| Criteria | Evaluation of Performance | | | Follow-up Assignments, Considerations |
	Unsatisfactory	Satisfactory	Outstanding	
Leadership				
defining the task				
disclosing parameters				
supporting the participants				
monitoring progress				
Individual(s) assigned to task				
expertise				
motivation				
contribution				
Group assigned to task				
task maturity of the group				
expertise of the group members				
creativity of the group members				
cohesiveness of the group				
"groupthink" tendency of group				
size of the group				
Resources				
time				
funds, facilities, equipment				
information/prof. development				
Quality of work product				

of the community that collective leadership is important and valued. Because such involvement requires preparation and professional development, it serves as a springboard for an active learning environment for adults as well as for students.

Figure 10.3 is an assessment tool for gathering the attitudes and opinions of participants regarding the quality of the school's *empowerment climate*. The thoughtful and inclusive school leader periodically involves the staff and community in assessing the environment in order to gauge the degree to which delegation is deemed to be effective and levels of empowerment are deemed to be appropriate.

FINALLY, TAKE ANOTHER LOOK IN THE MIRROR

Chapter 4 provided the opportunity to assess some of your dispositions as a leader. There's even a suggestion to ask a trusted colleague who knows you well to rate you according to the assessment items in Figures 4.2 (p. 44) and 4.4 (p. 49). With the material from subsequent chapters in mind, you can now consider a broader number of variables as you evaluate your dispositions toward effective delegation and empowerment. Figure 10.4 synthesizes the contingencies that were examined in Chapters 4 through 9, and provides the basis for a comprehensive assessment of a leader's ability to apply knowledge of the complex variables associated with delegation and empowerment.

Figure 10.5 (pp. 134–137) translates the delegation contingencies in Figure 10.4 into a comprehensive checklist and planning document that can be used to examine your readiness as a leader to delegate decisions and tasks. Analyze your knowledge of and willingness to employ these delegation contingencies in the process of empowering others to help accomplish the aims of your school. The first column describes leader behaviors in the six delegation contingency categories that were examined in Chapters 4 through 9. The second column invites you to assess your capacity in these performance areas by using a rating scale from 1 (low) to 5 (high). The third, fourth, and fifth columns can be used in those instances when you determine that your skill in a particular dimension is less than desirable. Column 3 asks you

(Text continues on page 137.)

FIGURE 10.3. ASSESSING SCHOOL CLIMATE: THE IMPACT OF DELEGATION AND EMPOWERMENT

Read the following statements. Circle the number at the right which best describes the degree to which you agree with the assertion in each statement.

1 - Agree Strongly
2 - Agree
3 - Not Sure
4 - Disagree
5 - Strongly Disagree

Impact on Individuals

The talents, interests, and expertise of individuals are utilized effectively in the school.   1   2   3   4   5

Individuals in this school fee valued, respected, and trusted.   1   2   3   4   5

Responsibility for decisions and tasks is apportioned fairly among staff and community members.   1   2   3   4   5

People are held accountable in appropriate ways for decisions and tasks which are delegated to them.   1   2   3   4   5

Individuals are recognized for their contributions to and successes with delegated decisions and tasks.   1   2   3   4   5

Impact on Teams

People enjoy participation in groups, committees, and teams.   1   2   3   4   5

Individuals in groups enthusiastically assist each other and work together to solve problems.   1   2   3   4   5

Teams manage conflict and complications well; quality is not sacrificed for the sake of harmony.   1   2   3   4   5

Teams are appropriately recognized for their successes, and share the credit with one another.   1   2   3   4   5

Impact on Climate

The atmosphere of the school is pleasant.	1	2	3	4	5
The involvement of others in planning, decision making, and tasks is valued.	1	2	3	4	5
Communication is clear and open among administrators, staff, parents, and students.	1	2	3	4	5
An air of mutual respect exists among administrators, staff, and community members.	1	2	3	4	5
Morale among school staff members, parents, and students is high.	1	2	3	4	5

Impact on Performance

The school community has a clear sense of the vision, goals, and major projects of the school.	1	2	3	4	5
Continuous learning and professional development of staff are valued within the school.	1	2	3	4	5
Data and other evidence document the success of delegated decisions and tasks.	1	2	3	4	5
People both internal and external to the school believe that the school is successful.	1	2	3	4	5

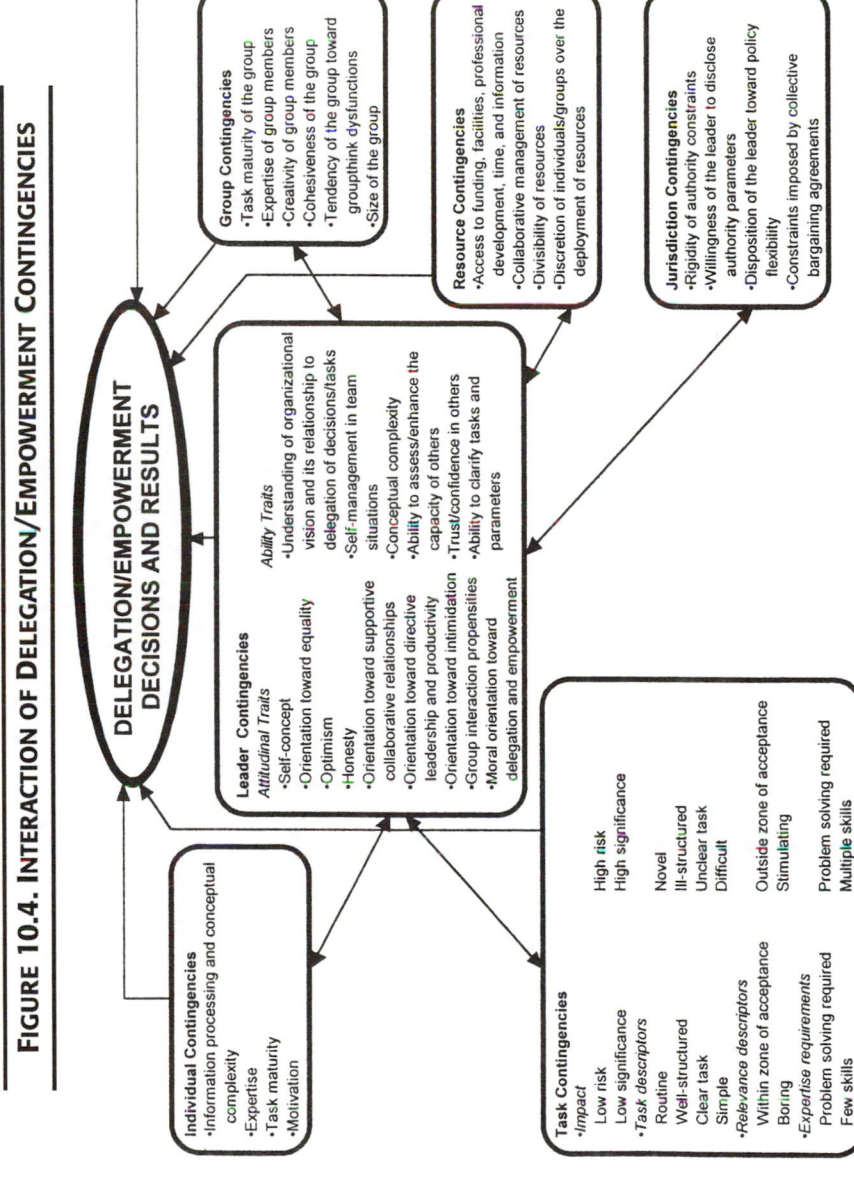

FIGURE 10.4. INTERACTION OF DELEGATION/EMPOWERMENT CONTINGENCIES

FIGURE 10.5. COMPREHENSIVE ASSESSMENT OF THE LEADER'S READINESS, WILLINGNESS, AND ABILITY TO DELEGATE AND TO EMPOWER OTHERS

1. Performance Dimension *Leadership Dimension*	2. Performance Quality (1=Low 5=High)	3. Motivation to Improve if Needed (1=Low 5=High)	4. Strategies for Learning	5. Other Leaders Who Can Assist
The leader:				
•Anchors decisions in a strong organizational vision				
•Exercises positive self-management in team situations				
•Possesses the necessary conceptual complexity				
•Is able to assess/enhance the capacity of others				
•Possesses trust/confidence in others				
•Is able to clarify tasks and parameters				
Task Dimension **The Leader:**				
•Is adept at analyzing the risk and significance of decisions/tasks				
•Is able to clarify a decision or task, and the degree to which it is novel, structured, clear, difficult				
•Accurately determines the degree to which the task is relevant to stakeholders				
•Assesses the level of expertise and skill that will be needed for decisions/tasks				

1. Performance Dimension	2. Performance Quality (1=Low 5=High)	3. Motivation to Improve if Needed (1=Low 5=High)	4. Strategies for Learning	5. Other Leaders Who Can Assist
Individual Dimension **The Leader:**				
•Is adept at assessing the information processing capacity and conceptual complexity of delegatees				
•Recognizes the expertise of potential participants				
•Assesses the degree of task maturity possessed by prospective delegatees				
•Is adept at gauging the motivation of prospective participants				
Group Dimension **The Leader:**				
•Assesses the degree of task maturity possessed by potential team				
•Recognizes expertise of prospective group members				
•Is adept at evaluating the creativity of potential group members				
•Assesses the cohesiveness of a group or team				
•Recognizes the tendency when a group develops "groupthink" dysfunctions				
•Is adept at gauging the appropriate size for a team depending upon the decisions/tasks to be completed				

1. Performance Dimension *Resource Dimension* **The Leader:**	2. Performance Quality (1=Low 5=High)	3. Motivation to Improve if Needed (1=Low 5=High)	4. Strategies for Learning	5. Other Leaders Who Can Assist
•Ensures that delegatees have access to necessary funding, facilities, professional development, time, and information				
•Collaborates in the management of resources				
•Accurately assesses the divisibility of resources				
•Appropriately delegates discretion over deployment of resources to individuals and groups				
Jurisdiction Dimension **The Leader:**				
•Assesses the rigidity of authority constraints				
•Consistently and willingly discloses authority parameters in advance				
•Is amenable to appropriate policy flexibility				
•Understands and acts within the constraints imposed by collective bargaining agreements				

to rate your motivation to develop the needed skills—if your response is closer to 5 (high motivation) than to 1 (low motivation), then column 4 invites you to develop some strategies by which you can strengthen performance in the particular skill area. If you are not particularly motivated to develop skills for a given performance dimension (your answer in column 3 is closer to 1 than to 5), then column 5 asks that you identify another (or others) in the school who can provide leadership for this performance dimension.

If you want to go a step further, ask an individual or a group of people with whom you work, preferably colleagues or subordinates, to anonymously assess you using columns 1 and 2. The implications of the responses for your own professional growth can be immeasurable.

The Moral Dimension of Delegation and Empowerment

Delegation and empowerment are valuable because of the potential benefit to the people in and associated with the school. Some may assume that this alone justifies any approach to delegation that a principal or other administrator may wish to employ. However, there are moral considerations that drive the use of these administrative tools. The basis for the moral dimension is a recognition of the rights of the stakeholder. This philosophy is founded on the notion that those affected significantly by the decisions and actions of administrators are entitled to be involved or represented in the process of making these decisions and of implementing related tasks.

In what ways is it evident that a leader understands the moral dimension of delegation and empowerment? The following sections outline some indicators that demonstrate the leader's commitment to the ethical use of these leadership tools.

Actions Speak Louder

The impact of the moral perspective cannot be overstated, for it drives the behavior of the school leader. The impact of such attitudes is evident in a number of specific leader behaviors and attitudes:

♦ Delegation and empowerment will not be employed just to make one's own life easier; nor will these administrative tools be used just to enhance personal power, avoid unpleasant tasks, or evade controversy. The moral leader will appreciate that, in addition to serving as tools for accomplishing organizational goals, delegation and empowerment are opportunities for building the capacity of individuals.

♦ The principal will consistently be attentive to the time, materials, equipment, space, and information needed by participants to carry out assigned decisions, planning, and tasks.

♦ Administrators will disclose constraints and parameters that limit the discretion, authority, and involvement of participants; even more, the school leader will work to remove such barriers. Authority constraints, where real, will not be overstated nor will potential flexibility with such constraints be withheld from participants.

♦ The school leader will avoid playing favorites among staff members, parents, and other stakeholders. While there are certainly those individuals who will frequently be called upon because of their skill and past performance, the wise and moral principal actively seeks to provide opportunities for others to develop capacity and demonstrate potential.

♦ Problems arising in the quality of decisions and tasks that have been delegated will be attributed first to problems in the process. Next, positive solutions will be sought; blaming participants will be the last and least frequently used response.

CREDIT WHERE CREDIT IS DUE

Individuals should be recognized when they work hard and perform assigned decisions and tasks well. In addition to compliments, expressions of gratitude, and formal commendations, these persons can be considered for job enrichment and mentoring opportunities, special assignments, special professional development, and promotions (Gullat & Bennett, 1995). The effort by leaders to demonstrate their appreciation is noted by those who accept responsibility for delegated decisions and tasks, and the performance and motivation of participants can be enhanced throughout the organization.

The ethical school leader will not seek or take credit at the expense of those who have helped to make progress possible. It is unfortunate that individuals who are in positions of authority often fail to recognize that the capacity to praise the contributions of others is perhaps the most praiseworthy action in which the leader can engage. Moreover, such behaviors are simply right and appropriate.

Drawing praise to one's self, and taking credit for the hard work of others, are among the most detested behaviors of those school leaders who fail to understand the moral dimension of delegation and empowerment. The ethical principal will give credit where credit is due; the principal will affirm the contributions of others, and find ways to celebrate the accomplishments of the school.

CONCLUSION

We began this text by acknowledging the growing complexity of school leadership. This complexity has been attended by the realization that it is neither possible nor desirable for school leaders to "do it all" when it comes to making and implementing decisions. Finding ways to manage the demanding workload in schools often requires that administrators assign decisions and tasks to others. Skills in delegation and perspectives on empowerment are increasingly necessary for principals and other administrators.

In recent years, school leadership has often been affected by a growing debate surrounding the opportunities provided for those most affected by the decisions and actions of administrators to have a significant role in shaping such policies and actions. Creating opportunities to share leadership and developing the skills and potential of others are additional reasons for administrators to develop their delegation skills. Leaders who become proficient in the processes of empowerment not only share power, they multiply it on behalf of their schools!

Throughout this text we have provided both a rationale for delegation and empowerment and an outline of those variables that most influence the administrator's ability to exercise these skills effectively. The examination of these variables and the application tools detailed in these chapters will assist you as you develop skills in delegation and including others in decisions and task completion.

APPLYING YOUR KNOWLEDGE

1. Assess the relative importance of the delegation contingencies.

   Review the delegation contingencies model described in Figure 10.4 (p. 133). Note that the contingency categories (leader, task, individual, group, resource, and jurisdiction) each impact effective delegation processes and results. It is also clear that the leader influences and impacts other contingency categories. With your colleagues or classmates, discuss the specific ways that you believe that the leader affects the other contingency categories, which in turn influence the effectiveness of delegation and empowerment. Support or challenge the notion that leadership is the most important of the factors related to delegation processes and results.

2. Tie it all together. Consider the interaction of delegation contingencies in the following vignette:

   At the October meeting, the Maysville Graded School District Board of Education voted to implement a plan to provide comprehensive mentoring support for all first and second year teachers. The plan will be developed in stages. First, principals will undergo extensive orientation to the key rationales for and components of mentoring programs. Second, a cadre of outstanding teachers from schools across the district will be selected. They will not only serve as the mentors, but they will also design the operational details of the program by the end of April. The Board will react to the proposed plan at the May meeting. Implementation of the plan is scheduled for the beginning of the coming school year.

With your classmates or colleagues, discuss and offer responses to the following:

- What decisions and tasks might the district administrators and principals delegate to others? Using the task descriptors from Chapter 5, how would you categorize each of these decisions and tasks?

- How do the theories and models undergirding the construct of task maturity help to explain the need for a mentoring program? How might these same theories inform the manner in which the principals work with and delegate responsibilities to the mentors in the early stages of the project?

- As the mentors undertake the summer planning process, what recommendations would you make to help them function productively as a group?

- What resources are likely to be of greatest value to principals and mentors during the planning phase, and as the project is undertaken and carried out?

- What constraints should be imposed on the authority of the mentors as they undertake both the planning and implementation of the project?

- How would you recommend that the district administrators and principals follow up on the decisions and tasks that have been delegated? In what manner should the outcomes of the decisions and tasks that were delegated be appraised?

3. Apply the appraisal criteria to delegation scenarios:

Consider the following delegated decisions and tasks. Consider the degree, in each instance, to which it would be valuable to conduct a followup and appraisal of the sort proposed in the form outlined in Figure 10.2 (p. 129).

- Conducting an annual summer planning/professional development retreat for faculty.
- Planning and implementing a community summit on business and school partnerships.
- Developing a new process for calculating high school grade-point average.

REFERENCES

Abdel-Halim, A. (1983). Effects of task and personality characteristics on subordinate responses to participative decision making. *Academy of Management Journal, 26* (3), 477–484.

Adams, S. (1963). Toward an understanding of inequity. *Journal of Abnormal Psychology, 67* (5), 422–436.

American Management Association (1984). How to delegate effectively. *Executive Skills, 7* (1), 1–16.

Armenta, A. & Reno, T. (1991). An administrator's self-esteem is key to effective delegation. *North Central Association Quarterly, 66* (3), 462–464.

Ashton, P. (1985). Motivation and the teacher's sense of efficacy. In C. Ames & R. Ames (Eds.), *Research on motivation in education, Vol. 2.* Orlando, FL: Academic Press, Inc.

Avolio, B., Alexander, R., Barrett, G., & Sterns, H. (1979). Analyzing preference for pace as a component of task performance. *Perceptual and Motor Skills, 49,* 667–674.

Baldwin, G. (1990). Collective negotiations and school site management. *West's Education Law Reporter, 58* (4), 1075–1083.

Barnard, C. (1938). *Functions of an executive.* Cambridge, MA: Harvard University Press.

Barrett, G. (1978). Task design, individual attributes, work satisfaction, and productivity. In A. Negandhi & B. Wilpert. (Eds.), *Work organization research: European and American perspectives.* Kent, OH: Kent State University Press.

Barth, R. (1987,March). *School: A community of leaders.* Paper presented at the annual spring institute of the Georgia State University Principals' Institute, Atlanta, GA. (ERIC Document Reproduction Service No. ED 281 277.)

Bem, D. J., Wallach, M. A., & Kogan, N. (1963). Group decision making under risk aversive consequences. *Journal of Personal and Social Psychology, 1,* 453–460.

Berliner, D. (1986). On the expert teacher: A conversation with David Berliner. *Educational Leadership, 44* (2), 4–9.

Blake, R. R., & Morton, J. S. (1985). *The managerial grid III.* Houston, TX: Gulf.

Blase, J. (1987). Dimensions of effective school leadership: The teacher's perspective. *American Educational Research Journal, 24,* 589–610.

Blase, J. & Kirby, P. (1992). *Bringing out The best In teachers: What effective principals do.* Newbury Park, CA: Corwin Press, Inc.

Bredeson, P. (1989, March). *Redefining leadership and the roles of school principals: Responses to changes in the professional work-life of teachers.* Paper presented at the annual meeting of the American Educational Research Association, San Francisco. (ERIC Document Reproduction Service No. ED 304 782.)

Bridges, E. (1967). A model for shared decision making in the school principalship. *Educational Administration Quarterly, 3,* 49–61.

Bryant, D. & MacPhail-Wilcox, B. (1988). A descriptive model of decision making: Review of idiographic influences. *Journal of Research and Development in Education, 22* (1), 7–22.

Burstein, E. & Vinokur, A. (1975). Persuasive argumentation and social comparison as determinants of attitude polarization. *Journal of Experimental Social Psychology, 13* (4), 315–332.

California Commission on Teacher Credentialing (1995). *Standards of quality and effectiveness for administrative services credential programs.* Sacramento, CA: California Department of Public Instruction.

Callaway, M. R. & Esser, J. K. (1984). Groupthink: Effects of cohesiveness and problem-solving procedures on group decision making. *Social Behavior and Personality, 12* (2), 157–164.

Carew, D., Parisi-Carew, E., & Blanchard, K. (1986). Group development and situational leadership: A model for managing groups. *Training and Development Journal, 40* (6), 46–50.

Conway, J. (1984). The myth, mystery, and mastery of participative decision making in education. *Education Administration Quarterly, 20* (3), 11–40.

Cooper, L. (1988). Stress coping preferences of principals. *NASSP Bulletin, 72* (509), 85–87.

Corcoran, T. & Wilson, B. (1985). *The secondary school recognition program: A first report on 202 high schools.* Philadelphia: Research for Better Schools, Inc.

Cuban, L. (1988). *The managerial imperative and the practice of leadership in schools.* Albany, NY: State University of New York Press.

Currie, G. & Rhodes, J. (1991, April). *Uncertainty and fragmentation: The "realities" of the principalship in the United States.* Paper presented at the annual meeting of the American Educational Research Association, Chicago. (ERIC Document Reproduction Service No. ED 332 362.)

Deming, W. E. (1986). *Out of the Crisis.* Cambridge, MA: MIT Center for Advanced Engineering Study.

Dixon, N. (1995). A practical model for organizational learning. *Issues and Observations 15* (2), 1–4.

Drucker, P. F. (1954). *The Practice of Management.* New York: Harper and Row.

Duke, D. (1994). Drift, detachment, and the need for teacher leadership. In D. Walling (Ed.) *Teachers as leaders: Perspectives on the professional development of teachers* (pp. 255–273). Bloomington, IN: Phi Delta Kappa Educational Foundation.

Duttweiler, P. C. & Mutchler, S. (1990). Harnessing the energy of people to improve schools. [Special Combined Issue] *Insights on Educational Policy and Practice Series.*

Dyer, W. G. (1983). *Contemporary Issues in Management and Organizational Development*. Reading, MA: Addison-Wesley.

Dykes, J. & Cooper, R. (1978). An investigation of the perceptual basis of redundancy gain and orthogonal interference for integral dimensions. *Perception and Psychophysics, 23* (1), 36–42.

Evans, C. & Dion, K. (1991). Group cohesion and performance: A meta-analysis. *Small Group Research, 22* (2), 175–186.

Fields, J. (1982). Principals and management training needs. *NASSP Bulletin, 66* (451), 36–40.

Finch, F. E. (1977). Collaborative leadership in work settings. *Journal of Applied Behavioral Science, 13* (3), 292–302.

Finn, C. (1992). *We must take charge: Our schools and our future.* New York: Maxwell MacMillan International.

Fisher, C. (1993). Boredom at work: A neglected concept. *Human Relations, 46* (3), 395–417.

Fleishman, E. (1978). Relating individual differences to the dimensions of human tasks. *Ergonomics, 21* (12), 1007–1019.

Frederick, C. (1993). In their own words: Qualities of effective middle level administrators. *School in the Middle, 3* (2), 25–28.

Fulk, J. & Wendler, E. (1982). Dimensionality of leader-subordinate interactions: A path-goal investigation. *Organizational Behavior and Human Performance, 30* (2), 241–264.

Gardner, D. (1986). Activation theory and task design: An empirical test of several new predictions. *Journal of Applied Psychology, 71* (3), 411–418.

Gastil, J. (1994). A definition and illustration of democratic leadership. *Human Relations, 47* (8), 367–377.

Getzels, J. & Guba, E. (1957). Social behavior and administrative process. *The School Review, 65* , 423–441.

Gips, C. & Bredeson, P. (1984, April). *The selection of teachers and principals: A model for faculty participation in personnel selection decisions in public schools.* Paper presented at the annual meeting of the American Educational Research Association, New Orleans,LA.(ERIC Document Reproduction Service No. ED 251 974).

Gray, B., O'Connor, S., & Decatur, M. (1994). The belief in equality inventory and leadership behavior: A construct validation. *Journal of Applied Social Psychology, 24* (4), 367–377.

Gronn, P. (1982). Neo-Taylorism in educational administration. *Educational Administration Quarterly, 18* (4), 17–35.

Gulick, L. (1937). Notes on the theory of organization. In L. Gulick & L. Urwick (Eds.). *Papers on the science of administration* (pp. 1–45). New York: Institute of Public Administration, Columbia University.

Gullatt, D. & Bennett, R. (1995). Motivational strategies useful in enhancing teacher performance. *NASSP Practitioner, 22* (2), 1–6.

Hackman, J. & Oldham, G. (1975). Development of the Job Diagnostic Survey. *Journal of Applied Psychology, 60* , 159–170.

Hackman, J. & Oldham, G. (1976). Motivation through the design of work: A test of a theory. *Organizational Behavior and Human Performance, 16,* 250–279.

Hallinger, P. (1992). The evolving role of American principals from managerial to instructional to transformational leaders. *Journal of Educational Administration, 30* (3), 35–47.

Halpin, A. W. (1966). *Theory and research in administration.* New York: McMillan.

Hedges, W. (1991). How do you waste time? *Principal, 71* (2), 37.

Hemphill, J. K. & Coons, A. E. (1950). *Leadership behavior description questionnaire.* Columbus, OH: Ohio State University.

Herman, J. (1991) *School-based management: Theory and practice* Reston, VA: National Association of Secondary School Principals.

Hersey, P. & Blanchard, K. (1977). *Management of organizational behavior: Utilizing human resources* (3rd ed.). Englewood Cliffs, NJ: Prentice-Hall.

Hersey, P. & Blanchard, K. (1982). *Management of organizational behavior: Utilizing human resources* (4th ed.). Englewood Cliffs, NJ: Prentice-Hall.

House, R. (1971). A path-goal theory of leader effectiveness. *Administrative Science Quarterly, 16* (3), 321–338.

House, R. & Mitchell, T. (1974). Path-goal theory and leadership. *Journal of Contemporary Business, 3*, 81–97.

Hoy, W. & Miskel, C. (1991). *Educational administration: Theory, research, and practice* (4th ed.). New York: McGraw-Hill.

Hoy, W. & Miskel, C. (1996). *Educational administration: Theory, research, and practice* (5th ed.). New York: McGraw-Hill.

Huddleston, J. Claspwell, M., & Killion, J. (1991). Participative decision making can capitalize on teacher expertise. *NASSP Bulletin, 75* (534), 80–89.

Imber, M. & Duke, D. (1984). Teacher participation in school decision making: A framework for research. *Journal of Educational Administration, 22* (1), 24–34.

Interstate School Leaders Licensure Consortium (1996). *Standards for School Leaders.* Washington, DC: Council of Chief State School Officers.

Isaacson, N. & Bamburg, J. (1992). Can schools become learning organizations? *Educational Leadership, 50* (3), 42–44.

Janis, I. (1982). *Groupthink: Psychological studies of policy decisions and fiascoes.* Boston: Houghton Mifflin.

Janis, I. (1985). Sources of error in strategic decision making. In J. Pennings (Ed.) *Organizational Strategy and Change.* San Francisco: Jossey-Bass.

Katz, R. (1978). The influence of job longevity on employee reactions to task characteristics. *Human Relations, 31* (8), 703–725.

Kelley, E. & Rodriguez, R. (1977). Observations on collective bargaining: Implications for academic management. *Liberal Education, 63* (1), 102–117.

Kerchner, C. (1979). The impact of collective bargaining on school governance. *Education and Urban Society, 11* (2), 181–207.

Kergaard, D. (1991). Time management: Handling it all. *NASSP Bulletin, 75* (533), 30–32.

Kimbrough, R. & Nunnery, M. (1988). *Educational administration.* New York: Macmillan.

King, B. & Kerchner, C. (1991, April). *Defining principal leadership in an era of empowerment.* Paper presented at the annual meeting of the American Research Association, Chicago, IL. (ERIC Document Reproduction Service No. ED 336 862)

Lacoursiere, R. B. (1980). *The life cycle of groups: Group development stage theory.* New York: Human Service Press.

Lay, C. (1992). Trait procrastination and the perception of person-task characteristics. *Journal of Social Behavior and Personality, 7* (3), 483–494.

Leana, C. (1985). A partial test of Janis' groupthink model: Effects of group cohesiveness and leader behavior on defective decision making. *Journal of Management, 11* (1), 5–17.

Leithwood, K. (1992). Transformational leadership: Where does it stand? *Education Digest, 58* (3), 17–20.

Lewis, J. (1987). *Recreating Our Schools for the 21st Century.* Westbury, NY: J. L. Wilkerson Publishing.

Lewis, J. (1989). *Implementing school-based management—by empowering teachers.* Westbury, NY: J. L. Wilkerson Publishing.

Lewis, J. (1990). *The James Lewis report on school-based management.* New York: The National Clearinghouse on School Based Management.

Lindquist, K. & Mauriel, J. (1989). School-based management: Doomed to failure? *Education and Urban Society, 21* (4), 403–415.

Liverpool, P. (1990). Employee participation in decision making: An analysis of the perceptions of members and non-members of quality circles. *Journal of Business and Psychology, 4* (4), 411–422.

Lyons, J. (1993). Perceptions of beginning public school principals. *Journal of School Leadership, 3* (2), 186–202.

MacPhail-Wilcox, B. & Alford, M. (1988). Restructuring schools and the teaching profession: What's the beef? *Voice, 3* (7), 30–31.

MacPhail-Wilcox, B., Forbes, R., & Parramore, B. (1990). Project design: Reforming structure and process. *Educational Leadership, 47* (7), 22–25.

Maeroff, G. (1993). Team building for school reform. *The School Administrator, 50* (3), 44–47.

Martin, O. (1990, November). *Instructional leadership behaviors that empower teacher effectiveness*. Paper presented at the annual meeting of the Mid-South Educational Research Association, New Orleans, LA. (ERIC Document Reproduction Service No. ED 327 513.)

Mayes, B. & Barton, M. (1987). Leader's behavior and subordinates' task percpetions: A multivariate investigation. *Perceptual and Motor Skills, 64* (3), 1171–1184.

McCall, J. (1994). *The principal's edge.* Larchmont, NY: Eye On Education.

McClelland, D. C. (1985). *Human motivation.* Glenview, IL: Scott, Foresman.

Mintzberg, H. (1973) *The nature of managerial work.* New York: Harper and Row,.

Miranda, S. (1994). Avoidance of groupthink: Meeting management using group support systems. *Small Group Research, 25* (1), 105–136.

Mohrman, A. M., Cooke, R. A., & Mohrman, S. A. (1978). Participation in decision making: A multidimensional perspective. *Educational Administration Quarterly,* 13–29.

Monk, B. et al. (1993). *Toward quality in education: The leader's odyssey.* Washington, DC: U.S. Dept. of Education, Office of Educational Research and Improvement.

Moracco, J., D'Arienzo, R., & Danforth, D. (1983). Comparison of teachers who are contented and discontented in their career choices. *Vocational Guidance Quarterly, 32* (1), 44–51.

Mullen, B. & Copper, C. (1994). The relation between group cohesiveness and performance: An integration. *Psychological Bulletin, 115* (2), 210–227.

Mullen, B., Anthony, T., Salas, E., & Driskell, J. (1994). Group cohesiveness and quality of decision making: An integration of tests of the groupthink hypothesis. *Small Group Research, 25* (2), 189–204.

Murphy, J. (1994a). *Principles of school-based management.* Chapel Hill, NC: North Carolina Educational Policy Research Center.

Murphy, J. (1994b). Redefining the principalship in restructuring schools. *NASSP Journal, 78* (560), 94–99.

Muse, I., Hite, S., Smith, R., Matthews, J., & Britsch, C. (1993). Delegation. In S. Thomson (Ed.), *Principals for our changing schools: Knowledge and skill base* (pp. 7-1–7-24). National Policy Board for Educational Administration. Lancaster, PA: Technomic.

Ordidge, P. (1985). Delegation—is it different for managers in education? *Educational Management and Administration, 12,* 13–16.

Peters, T. & Waterman, R. (1982). *In search of excellence.* New York: Harper and Row.

Pitner, N. (1988). The study of administrator effects and effectiveness. In N. Boyan (Ed.) *Handbook of research on educational administration* (pp. 99–122). New York: Longman.

Pitner, N. & Ogawa, R. (1981). The school superintendent: A case of organizational leadership. *Educational Administration Quarterly, 17* (2), 45–65.

Plunkett, D. (1990). The creative organization: An empirical investigation of the importance of participation in decision making. *Journal of Creative Behavior, 24* (2), 140–148.

Principal and Administrator Professional Standards Board (1994). *Standards for school principals in Colorado.* Denver, CO: Colorado Department of Education.

Puffer, S. (1989). Task-completion schedules: Determinants and consequences for performance. *Human Relations, 42* (10), 937–955.

Roberts, N. & Bradley, R. (1991). Stakeholder collaboration and innovation: A study of public policy initiation at the state level. *Journal of Applied Behavioral Science, 27* (2), 209–227.

Sato, K. (1988). Trust and group size in a social dilemma. *Japanese Psychological Research, 30* (2), 88–93.

Schaaf, D. (1991, March). Beating the drum for quality. *Training, the Magazine of Human Resource Development,* 5, 6, 8, 11, 12, 30.

Schneider, G. T. (1984). Teacher involvement in decision making: Zones of acceptance, decision conditions, and job satisfaction. *Journal of Research and Development in Education, 18* (1), 25–32.

Schroder, H. M., Driver, M. J., & Streufert, S. (1967). *Human information processing.* New York: Holt, Reinhart, and Winston.

Scott, C. & Jaffe, D. (1991). *Empowerment: A practical guide for success.* Los Altos, CA: Crisp Publications, Inc.

Seeley, D. (1991, April). *Brother can you paradigm? Finding a banner around which to rally in restructuring schools.* Paper presented at the annual meeting of the American Educational Research Association, Chicago, IL. (ERIC Document Reproduction Service No. ED 333 541)

Shaw, K. (1990). Putting sociology into practice. *Wisconsin Sociologist, 27* (2–3), 12–17.

Simon, H. (1947). *Administrative behavior.* New York: Mac-Millan.

Smith, S. C. (1981). *School leadership: Handbook for survival.* ERIC Clearinghouse on Educational Administration. (ERIC Document Reproduction Service No. ED 209 736)

Sousa, D. (1982). What ever happened to shared decision making? *NASSP Bulletin, 66* (456), 53–56.

Stoner, J. A. (1961). *A comparison of individual and group decisions involving risk.* Unpublished master's thesis. Cambridge, MA: Massachusetts Institute of Technology, School of Industrial Management.

Taylor, R. & Card, R. (1985). *Power sown, power reaped.* Augusta, ME: Felicity Press.

Thomas, W.C. (1989). Delegation—a skill necessary in school-based management. *NASSP Bulletin, 73* (518), 30–32.

Thomson, S. D. (Ed.) (1993). *Principals for our changing schools: Knowledge and skill base.* National Policy Board for Educational Administration. Lancaster, PA: Technomic.

Tuckman, B. (1965). Developmental sequence in small groups. *Psychological Bulletin, 63* (6), 384–399.

Tuckman, B. & Jensen, M. (1977). Stages of small group development revisited. *Group and Organization Studies, 2* (4), 419–427.

Tye, K. (1993). Going beyond the rhetoric of restructuring schools. *The Education Digest, 58* (6), 4–7.

Tyler, T. (1991). Using procedures to justify outcomes: Testing the viability of a procedural justice strategy for managing conflict and allocating resources in work organizations. *Basic and Applied Social Psychology, 12* (3), 259–279.

Vroom, V. (1964). Work and motivation. New York: Wiley.

Vroom, V. & Yetton, P. (1973). Leadership and decision making. Pittsburgh, PA: University of Pittsburgh Press.

Walton, M. (1986). *The Deming management method*. New York: Putnam.

Ward, M. (1996). New standards for the preparation and licensure of school administrators. *Voice, 8* (1), 31–33.

Watson, C. (1983, August). Motivational effects of feedback and goal setting on group performance. Paper presented at the annual convention of the American Psychological Association, Anaheim, CA. (ERIC Document Reproduction Service No. ED 243 001)

Webster, W. (1994). Teacher empowerment in a time of great change. In D. Walling (Ed.) *Teachers as leaders: perspectives on the professional development of teachers* (pp. 103–117). Bloomington, IN: Phi Delta Kappa Educational Foundation.

Wheelan, S. & McKeage, R. (1993). Developmental patterns in large and small groups. *Small Group Research, 24* (1), 60–83.

White, P. (1974). Resources as determinants of organizational behavior. *Administrative Science Quarterly, 19* (3), 366–379.

White, P. (1989). An overview of school-based management: What does the research say? *NASSP Journal, 73* (518), 1–8.

Wofford, J. C. & Srinivasan, T. N. (1983). Experimental tests of the leader-environment-follower-interaction theory of leadership. *Organizational Behavior and Human Performance, 32* (1), 35–54.

Wohlstetter, P. & Odden, A. (1992). Rethinking school-based management policy and research. *Educational Administration Quarterly, 28* (4), 529–549.

Wolcott, H. (1973). *The man in the principal's office.* New York: Holt, Rinehart, and Winston.

Yeaman, A. (1994). Fair assignment of responsibilities. *Tech Trends, 39* (4), 17.